Young Widow: A Memoir

by Sarah Wauterlek

ISBN: 0615543367

ISBN-13: 9780615543369

Young Widow: *A Memoir*

A journal of the first year after the death of a spouse

Introduction

My memoir captures the details of the year following the death of my husband, Mark. I understand that my recollections may not align with those of others who were there, as perceptions can differ. The thoughts and feelings that I write about are what I felt and experienced and perceived to be true at that time. I am grateful that I have come out of that intense grief and I'm grateful to my families, the Carlsons and the Wauterleks, who through the difficulty of grief have chosen to support each other in love. It's been a difficult journey, as it still is, since we continue to miss Mark so very much.

It certainly doesn't seem as though life is ever perfectly clear. Just when we think it is, death comes unexpectedly in one of its many forms, and life as we once knew it to be no longer exists for us. Life cannot be controlled. One of humanity's greatest disillusions is that we think we can truly control our lives. For me, the most freeing point in living has come from learning how to live with an open hand, for I now know that I cannot hold on to anyone or anything. They are not mine. Nothing is. It all belongs to our Creator.

"It is a fearful thing to love what death can touch."– Anonymous

Senseless Living

The caress of your hand on the top of mine as I drink in the sweet warmth of belonging to someone so wonderful, of belonging to you.
An idealistic future.
The false illusion of feeling safe and secure.
Seeing life's possibilities as just that: endless possibilities.
The warmth of life growing inside of me and ultimately becoming the physical representation of our love.
These are now lost to me, buried six feet below—along with you.

I don't hate you for leaving me; I know it was not your choice. You wouldn't have left me this way.

But how now can I go on living? Living a life defined by loss and pain? Where is the comfort that I had found only with you?

I long to be touched; oh, how I long to be embraced and held! And yet, when others try, it only causes me to recoil within. Their comfort comes nowhere near the depths of me. Is there no release from the pain? Where are your hands, my love? They are the only ones that can heal me now.

I desperately hold on to the facade of composure that I portray. If I allow myself to truly feel the loss of it all, I may never recover. How can I endure this suffocating burden of grief and loneliness?

The pain is too much. I feel as though I cannot endure it. Yet, I have no choice. No choice.

I will live with this pain. I will live without you. I will live and hope to find breathing easier in time. I will live and hope to find you in my dreams. I will live waiting for the day that you meet me upon my final breath and welcome me into heaven. You will welcome me home.

1. Age Misconceptions

I'm thirty years old, but on the outside I appear to others to be in my early to mid twenties. Yet on the inside I feel like I'm closer to eighty. What is age then? The obvious answer is that age represents how long someone has lived—years made up of months, days, hours, minutes, and seconds. However, most of us view it as so much more. Age represents how we should look, the kinds of experiences we should have had, and the life that we should be currently living. For example, many thirty-year-old women expect to be married with children (or have plans for them soon) or have successful careers—or both. At thirty, a woman will have made it through the self-discovery years of her twenties and will hopefully have a better idea of who she is as a result. The twenties are full of questions and figuring out what to do with life. By the time a woman reaches thirty, she is expected to be secure with a stronger identity of self. At thirty, people assume that if she isn't married, she hasn't been "lucky in love," as they say, or she's been too busy pursuing her career.

When strangers look at me and see the absence of a diamond ring, they ask, "Why aren't you married yet?" No one looks at me, a young-looking thirty-year-old, and thinks that perhaps I am a widow. They don't know that I once had the things that a thirty-year-old should have. My reality blows away preconceived notions about what someone my age should be experiencing. I've experienced too much to be so young. I find that I embody the representation of three ages: twenty-five is how old I look, thirty is the number of years I've had, and eighty more accurately represents the word *widow* that is now bestowed upon me.

2. Eulogies from the funeral:

My Eulogy (read by my sisters)

Sunday, May 6, 2007

Mark,
You are supposed to be coming home today, and I find myself anxiously awaiting your return. I can see your smile and I can feel your loving embrace as you enter our back door while dropping your bag full of rumpled clothes and fishing equipment on the floor. It probably smells, and I'm sure it will stay there for a couple of days until you finally put it away. You would say, "I missed you so much," and you would kiss me by the kitchen counter as Bristol would wiggle her way between us, licking your hands, clothes, everything. You would go on to tell me the stories of your adventurous trip as if you were the luckiest guy in the world. If I would try to pull away after a while, you would pull me closer, smile, and say, "Don't you want to love me?" So I would stay in your arms and listen, and the scene would play out as it has so many times before.

You always had such great adventures, Mark, and we would laugh at the opportunities that came to you. It wasn't always as clear to me then as it is now that you made so many of those opportunities happen. You knew, more than most, how to make time for friends and family. You lived life, and you never sat still. You knew how to prioritize your life. And Mark, although there were times, like this one, when I wanted to selfishly keep you at home with me, I knew how happy you were to go, and I loved you too much to deny you that. I also know that had I asked, you would have stayed, because you would have done anything for me. I never once felt second-best in your life.

People have been asking me how we left each other on Thursday morning, and I smile when I think about it. I think about how you stood above me as you woke me with a kiss. I turned over to see you in one of your outdoorsman outfits that you have probably owned for years and may never have washed. You told me with that goofy smirk on your face that you had stayed up late to book our trip to Turkey and Greece. As I watched a smile spread across your handsome face, I knew that smile was more about how happy you had made me than how happy you were about the trip. Mark, you were so amazing that way, and your overwhelming generosity was only one of your wonderful qualities. You were also intelligent, humble, loving, committed, faithful, and trustworthy. I am so proud of who you were—you were truly a man of God. I am forever grateful for the many ways your presence in my life has made me a better person.

Your friends and family are here, and somehow it makes me feel excited, as if they were here to help us celebrate our wedding. How ironic. But Mark, when I think about the truth of why they are here, there are so many tears, and I find that I have to tell myself to breathe. I know you would have never wanted to leave me like this, leave your family like this, and leave your friends like this. You loved us so much, and you always did everything to bring joy to people's lives. I wish you could know just how much happiness you brought into the lives of those around you. I find that there are no words to describe your worth. You truly were a gift from God, as you were as close to perfect as I could have ever imagined. I would never have believed that I could love and be loved so much as with you. Mark, I have no regrets with you. I lived the ten best years of my life with you, and I am grateful to know that I loved you with everything within me, and that you felt that. Oh, Mark, although sometimes I have no idea how Jesus is going to get me through this terrible pain that I feel, I know he will, because he is faithful. Mark, you brought me incredible joy in this life, and I am anxiously waiting to be reunited with you again in heaven.

I love you so very much,
Sarah

Ben's Eulogy

Many of you know me as "Benny." I knew Mark as "Leeky," "Leeks," "Wauterbuckets," "Wauterlove," and "Wauterdog." Mark was my best friend on the planet. In the brief moments shortly after hearing of Mark's death, and in a state of shock, I must have said something to Sarah about wanting to speak . . . 'cause here I am. Sarah, thank you for giving me this moment.

I met Mark in the summer of 1998. Over the past nine years, Mark has been my friend, my confidant, my soul mate, and my coconspirator in countless adventures: chasing fish, hunting, and just living life. Before Mark and Sarah moved to Chicago, we had weekly sushi outings, followed by movies or video games, or both, depending on what Sarah would let Mark and me do. We'd stay up late into the evening, and Sarah would fall asleep on the couch while Mark and I duked it out on some of the finest golf courses in the world, living vicariously through Tiger Woods and Jesper Parnevik. Six o'clock a.m. would come so painfully early. I'd be hating life, and Mark would be excitedly consumed with the thought of stalking monster trout on the rush. We'd have an epic morning on the river, Mark would catch more fish than me, and I'd pout. Then he'd come to my rescue and put every bit of his knowledge and form into my casts to ensure my own success. We'd return home for an afternoon nap and throw in some girlie movie Sarah picked out. Mark would fall asleep within ten minutes, and I'd get sucked into some sappy story with Sarah. The day would turn to evening, and I'd start dropping hints that I should probably go so Mark and Sarah could have some time together in their first year of marriage . . . rarely would I get out of there before midnight.

It would take me days to share all the stories and to quantify the impact Mark has had on my life. And as I look around this room, I realize that days could turn into months if each of you had a moment to share. It's my hope as I stand here before you that my words do justice to your memories.

Based on the many conversations I've had with others who knew and loved Mark, I'm highlighting pieces of Mark's character that most of you will recognize:

Mark was selfless. He put others first. I can't tell you how many times we'd be hunting or fishing when he would prioritize my experience. He always made sure others were having a good time; he made sure others were fishing in the best spots. He would be tying flies for the group, testing flies on stubborn fish, and leading others to the promised land of trout in hand. This isn't just a fishing story, though—he wanted others to be successful and was constantly counseling others, connecting people in the business world, grabbing a paintbrush to help friends paint the walls of their homes (although some may have wished he didn't), or helping others rip out their lawns and reshape their landscape. He was an assistant and helper in the daily events of our lives.

Mark was adventurous and lived with reckless abandon. He couldn't sit still. He was the catalyst and anchor for so many of the epic adventures in all our lives. He organized the trips. He lived life fully and rarely said no. Last Tuesday I talked to him, and he said, "I know you are gonna hate me, but I'll be fishing the Bear Trap Canyon Friday." I gave him a decent scolding for the no-invite, but at the end I said, "Eh, I still love you tons." And he said, "Yeah, I love you too, buddy." Mark was always the first to wade across a treacherous river crossing, blast 330-yard drives straight over water in an attempt to reach the green well ahead of his friends, and never afraid to launch off a cliff on his snow skis while Sarah and I cautiously watched from below. He lived life to the fullest, and he did it with graceful and reckless abandon.

Mark was humble. He downplayed everything to the point of lying—you would ask him how many fish he caught, and you'd get a very ambiguous answer: "Oh, I don't know, a couple." But you saw him catch a dozen with your own eyes. He didn't want the attention; he didn't need to be at the center. But he was.

Mark lived to share eternal life with others. Mark and I had countless talks about the salvation and well-being of our friends. He spoke often about what we could do to have a significant impact with eternal consequences in the lives of those we interacted with. Sometimes those conversations were about close friends and sometimes they were about complete strangers.

I feel a tremendous void in my life—it is hard to imagine how I can face the next phase of life without Mark. From the very first moment I received the news last Thursday, I felt as though half of my body and soul just died.

When I arrived Saturday and first saw Mark's parents, John and Vicky, I could barely stand. I was weeping in John's arms, and he comforted me and whispered something to me that gives me great strength and hope.

He said, "Ben, it could have been you, or it could have been me. We never know when our time is up. God gave me thirty wonderful years of life with Mark. The only thing we can do is live our lives in a way that makes a difference in other people's lives . . . so that when we are gone, others can carry on in that very same fashion."

John, Vicky—well done. That is exactly how your son lived. I am standing here, on behalf of everyone gathered, as living proof that you succeeded in raising Mark. He had an incredible impact on me. He had an incredible impact on everyone sitting here surrounding you. Sarah, you so selflessly shared your husband with all of us. The pain I feel in my heart for you, for the grief and sorrow that you will endure, is greater than anything I have felt in my entire life. Mike, your brother was an amazing human being, and I don't say this to you lightly: I love you like I loved your brother.

I've been thinking a lot about how I will ever fill the void in my heart and soul that Mark has left. The only glimmer of hope and spark of redemption I can wrap my arms around in the midst of this great tragedy is that I know that God's gracious healing power and strength can graft the quality, character, and spirit of Mark into my own heart. God can graft how he lived onto how I live, and I can go forward with the reckless abandon that he did to make an eternal difference in the lives of those who will succeed me. And I will hope and pray that we all will be encouraged to live with the humility, selflessness, and the kind of adventure that Mark embodied in all that he did.

Doug's Eulogy

Reflections on Mark

These past several days, I've found myself going back to a particular moment that I shared with Mark. I can close my eyes and I'm right there. We're riding in his truck, it's the spring of our senior year in college, and we're on our way to another afternoon of mountain-biking adventure at Battle Creek Park in Saint Paul. We've got Joe Diffie playing on the stereo. We're laughing so hard, it's hard to keep the car on the road. His hair is a mess and a bit overdue for a haircut, and he's sporting a two-day beard that I know I couldn't grow in two weeks. Our future lies ahead of us. Everything is right. I love going back there; I don't want to leave.

There are other places I've gone back to in my mind: intensely competitive floor hockey games in the basement of our college rental house, morning trips to Caribou Coffee to talk and pray together, paintball matches leaving us all covered in welts, repeated screenings of *Braveheart* (which would usually put him to sleep within the first seven minutes), grilling the meat he had recently killed, and the ski trips we took together to Montana and Colorado. I'm sure most of you have closed your eyes and have been flooded with wonderful memories of Mark too, and they've brought smiles and laughter through the tears that have defined these past six days.

But outside of these adventures and the high points, what was it that defined Mark? What did he convey with the way he lived his life? What were the characteristics that made him the wonderful friend, husband, brother, and son that he so clearly was? What would he want us to remember him by? I'd like to share a few of my thoughts with you that I think start to answer these questions.

Mark was a devoted husband. Sarah, I remember when I found out that you and Mark had started dating. Being your cousin, I was inclined to be a bit protective of you, and was glad to be able to keep tabs on things when you decided to come to Bethel. But hearing that you and Mark were together set me at ease. I knew Mark would treat you with respect and as a gentleman. As your relationship grew and resulted in marriage, that proved so true.

Sarah, I can't tell you of all the times he bragged about you when you weren't around. He loved you so much, and you were such a wonderful wife to him. Proverbs 12:4 says, "A worthy wife is her husband's joy and crown." I can't think of a more fitting analogy of how he treasured you and how you brought so much happiness into his life. You truly were Mark's joy and his crown.

Mark was an intensely loyal guy. He was a man's man, and he loved his friends deeply. Again drawing from Proverbs, this time chapter 17, verse 17: "A friend is always loyal, and a brother is born to help in time of need." This was a consistent feature of his life. I saw Mark do little things, like supporting a friend going through hard times by watching his dog. My wife and I experienced this support in bigger ways when we have gone on missions trips, and he and Sarah have prayed for us and helped us. He always noticed when people were struggling and needing encouragement, and went out of his way to walk alongside them.

Mark was easygoing and made those around him feel welcome and comfortable. Everyone loved Mark, save those times when you were matched up against him in floor hockey. His warmth and genuine down-to-earth personality were always on display. He lived in the moment and invested deeply in relationships. Looking out at you today, I know many of you counted him as a dear friend. He gave generously with his love and laughter, and our lives are all richer because of it.

But underlying all this, the framework that Mark's character was built upon was his relationship with and love for Jesus Christ. Thank you, John, Vicky, and Mike for instilling these values into him and for allowing each of us to share in enjoying the man he became. I love the 3rd chapter of Colossians, and the 16th and 17th verses were so evident in Mark's life: "Let the words of Christ, in all their richness, live in your hearts and make you wise. . . . And whatever you do or say, let it be as a representative of the Lord Jesus, all the while giving thanks through him to God the Father." Simply put, this is what Mark was about and what he would want us to remember him by.

Mark, we take great joy and comfort in knowing that you are now with the Savior for eternity. But our sorrow at our loss is beyond anything words can begin to express. We will never forget you. Thank you for being a part of our lives. We love you, Mark, and we'll miss you so much.

Mike's Eulogy

I know that Mark was a brother to many of you, so much of what I say will more than likely just reaffirm what you already know about him. For those of you who didn't know Mark all that well, much of what I say might sound exaggerated or far-fetched, but Mark was my best friend, big brother, and a role model all in one, so things are bound to seem that way. I'm also positive that if you talked to Mark's many other brothers that are here right now, they would tell you similar things or perhaps even add to what I have to say.

Mark was about as close to perfection as I have ever seen in a human being. I can't say that I ever saw Mark get mad or angry, stressed out or overwhelmed. One of the many conversations I've had about Mark over the last few days that really struck me was about his demeanor on the golf course. One of Mark's friends was talking about how they never saw him yell or throw a golf club out of frustration while playing one of life's most frustrating games, and it really got me thinking. As practically a scratch golfer, why would someone be frustrated playing a game they were nearly perfect at? This thought provoked a later discussion I had with my mom and dad in which we tried to think of something that Mark wasn't really, really good at. After some thought and discussion, we came up with nothing. Mark weighed fifty pounds less than me but could hit a golf ball a hundred yards farther than me. Mark was one of the smartest, one of the most athletic, and one of the most likeable people I know, and, despite all these things, one of the most humble people I know. Mark was never negative and always had a kind word for any friend or stranger alike in a world that thrives on negativity. Mark was the kind of guy that if you had a problem with him or something that he did, it was more than likely true that you were the one who had the problem in reality. Even though Mark was attending Kellogg and working on many very time-intensive real-estate deals, he would always bend over backward to answer any question I might have or to use his influence to help me succeed as I began my career in real estate. Mark was an avid outdoorsman, as you can tell from the many photos you can see around. By looking at the photos, you might guess that Mark spent every second of his life enjoying the outdoors. While this wasn't totally true, it doesn't mean that Mark wouldn't have liked it to be that way. Mark's idea of a perfect day would be hanging out in a tree stand or a duck blind, or floating down a Montana river with a fly rod in hand alongside my dad or one of his many other friends who just never seemed to catch half the fish that Mark did. Mark's idea of a perfect night would be spent watching football or UFC with friends and family while eating pizza and, of course, red licorice or gummy bears for dessert.

Mark's perfection even extended to his love life. Mark only dated one girl in his life, and he married that girl. This type of success in dating is very rare these days. It wasn't only that he dated one girl and married her, but that this girl was truly so perfect for him. I have never seen two better friends than Mark and Sarah or a couple that lived in such harmony as Mark and Sarah, with such an understanding of who each other was and what each other needed. One of the true pleasures I've had in my life was living with Mark and Sarah for three months last summer. In those three months it became abundantly clear to me that Sarah really did love Mark, as she put up with my various antics and embraced me as a brother. I had the chance to witness true love firsthand. I remember thinking that Mark and Sarah were the perfect role models of what a husband and wife should be, and what marriage should be.

Mark's role model in life was my dad. Our dad's unique outlook on life and his love for the Lord is something both Mark and I greatly admired. On one occasion recently, Mark and I had discussed how Dad's life has been a true testament to what faith in God really means. Our dad's unwavering faith and strength through this time of crisis is something that I know Mark would have great pride in, and it is something that will surely serve as a cornerstone to my beliefs for the rest of my life.

In many ways, Mark's hero was our mom. Mark was amazed at Mom's dedication to improving the lives of those less fortunate and to spreading the Word of God. Mom's zeal for God was something we both envied. Mark planned on becoming more involved with Mom's tireless work toward adding to God's kingdom.

Most of all, Mark loved his family and friends, and he loved God. Mark's desire to follow God's will was evident in all his actions, and he was blessed accordingly. Mark's accomplishments in his thirty years surpassed what many would hope to achieve in a lifetime. Today and the many tomorrows to follow will no doubt be filled with grieving the loss of a friend, a brother, a son, and a husband. But for all these reasons, I say we celebrate Mark's life.

Dr. William Washington's Address

My name is Dr. William Washington, and six years ago I had the privilege of officiating the wedding of Mark and Sarah. I've been a family friend for fifteen years.

As mentioned, I was there to witness the joining together of these two beautiful families through the union of Mark and Sarah. We met together that day to celebrate under the banner of joy, but today we meet together to grieve this unspeakable and sudden loss under the banner of hope. The lives of these two families were forever bound together that day through marital love and affection, but now they are forever bound together in shared memory and legacy of a beloved son and faithful husband.

Grief is not all that binds us together today, however, because as followers of the risen Christ, we do not grieve as those who have no hope. Because we gather together in the name of the suffering Christ, we have confidence that our grief and pain do not fall on deaf ears in the throne room of heaven, and because we gather together in the name of the risen Christ, we're able grieve as he has promised, as those who have hope. So, this great company gathers here today to remember and reflect upon the legacy of Mark's life, lived as a follower of Jesus Christ.

We've gathered here together today to give thanks to the Lord for a life well lived. I've been to a couple services in my life where people got up and said some things about people, and you had the sense that there was a little character inflation going on. But anybody who knew John Mark knows that there is no need to inflate the goodness of his character. When people stop to remember the life of somebody who truly had good character, the best thing to do is to just step back and let his life speak. So, what we want to do right now is tell some stories that let the character of Christ, as manifested through the life of Mark, challenge and encourage us to live a life worthy of the calling of Jesus Christ. I just want to share one story with you that illustrates the depth and quality of this young man's character.

In many ways, I was also Mark's daddy. I was his barbecue daddy. I taught Mark how to barbeque, marinade, season, and peel baby back ribs. There is a very intricate, confidential, and complicated way of preparing Coff Dog's ribs. Mark was my Jedi apprentice, eager to learn and teach. It's interesting that one day, the apprentice became the teacher.

It happened the first time that I went hunting with Mark and his dad. And when I mean hunting, I mean with a shotgun. First of all, I had never fired a firearm or shotgun before. And, there's good reason: because they don't build them small enough to fit a body like mine. The first time I took a shot, the butt of the gun hit me flush in the jaw. My teeth were rattling after the first shot. I remember going to the firing range to shoot the clay pellets so that I could later shoot pheasants. I think I hit one out of fifty. My shoulder was throbbing; I felt a bit uncomfortable and embarrassed, and I knew I was costing them money because I was missing so often.

I remember Mark coming over to me, anticipating how I was feeling. He didn't take the time to make fun of me, but he took the time to reassure me. He didn't highlight my shortcomings or the fact that I missed so many, but how I hit one—and, if I hit one, I could hit others. Later that day, I was successful in shooting more than one pheasant. Mark, as he has done for so many of us, saw the good in my life, and that is what he would speak to. He had an uncanny ability to make us feel special and to feel loved. He gained his qualities from his upbringing—from the love he received from his father and mother. He learned that we're all precious in God's sight. Mark loved everybody, never looking at his or her financial, educational, or racial composition. He loved life, the outdoors, hunting and fishing with his father, holding and hugging his wife, barbecuing ribs, and giving comfort and encouragement to his friends.

I'll always remember that day on the hunting range, where he rejoiced with me, and the times we shared together barbecuing ribs (for which now I understand that 99 percent of his friends know the secret recipe!). Whether he was my student or my teacher, I will never forget Mark's unassuming style and grace, his gift of encouragement, and how he would constantly leave a smile on my face.

Committal- Dr. William Washington

We have entrusted our brother Mark to God's mercy,
And now we commit his mortal remains to the ground:
Earth to earth, ashes to ashes, dust to dust:
In sure and certain hope of the resurrection to eternal life
Through our Lord Jesus Christ,
Who will transform our frail bodies that they may be
Conformed to his glorious body,
Who died, was buried, and rose again for us.
To him be the glory forever.
Amen

May 3, 2007

I've never been very good at remembering specific dates. Unfortunately, May 3, 2007, is a date that I will never forget. May 3rd is the day that my husband, Mark, died. May 3, 2007, is the day that I wished I had died too.

I met and fell in love with Mark at the end of my freshman year in college. We dated for four years before getting married on July 28, 2001, and I enjoyed almost six years of marriage with him. Our life together was close to idyllic. We were in love and enjoyed so much of what the world had to offer. Mark was incredibly handsome, intelligent, kind, humble, generous, adventurous, and successful. His career afforded us the opportunity to purchase a beautiful home, enjoy many evenings out at wonderful restaurants, and travel extensively. It was largely because of this that we had decided to put off trying for a family of our own until later in life. We were enjoying our time together in these years of our youth, and because we could afford to travel as much as we did, we thought we would wait to have children. Life was beautiful and full of opportunity.

I knew I was extremely lucky, and I often wondered why I had been given so much when others had so little. I can wholeheartedly say that I envied no other life, and I thought that because I was so grateful for what I had, God wouldn't take it from me. My glass-half-full, idealistic mentality couldn't comprehend what happened then on May 3, 2007. I lived in that state of shock for a long time as this incomprehensible grief shattered my contented state of being. It shattered my soul and my heart.

May 3, 2007, was a Thursday. Mark was going to Montana for a long weekend with his boss. He had been asked to go on a fishing trip with a group of older, successful businessmen, and he was excited for many reasons. First of all, Mark loved fly-fishing more than just about anything else, and he especially loved fishing in Montana. He loved the crisp air, rugged land, and peace found in nature coupled with the adrenaline of chasing trout. Secondly, he was excited about the opportunity to spend time with older, accomplished businessmen and to learn from them. He had a way of fitting in with older generations, and he was anxious to take advantage of any wisdom that they might impart to him. Perhaps most importantly, Mark was extremely excited to fly in his boss's private jet. He had recently been talking about taking flying lessons and even someday purchasing his own plane. Some of the other men in the office had their pilot licenses, and Mark had hoped to one day obtain his own. I can still remember him spending many nights on the couch with his laptop, looking at planes to purchase as we would watch TV together. With great enthusiasm, he would turn to show me the planes he had found, and I would respond by saying he had to wait until he could buy an expensive-enough one, like his boss's, so that it would be safer. How ironic it is to think of my statement now.

Truth be told, I didn't want Mark to go on the trip. Selfishly, I had wanted him to stay. I had never liked being at home alone at night, and even though I had made plans of my own with friends, I wanted to be with him more than with anyone else. I loved spending time with my husband, and I knew I would miss him. We enjoyed being together, but we were also good about taking a balanced approach to life by letting each other do our own things. Mark was my best friend, and I missed him when he was away. However, we both believed it was healthy to allow each other to pursue our own interests and to spend quality time with friends. It made our marriage stronger . . . and that is why I didn't ask him to stay. *Oh Lord, how I have wished that I could go back and beg him, plead with him, to stay. He would have if I had asked. How was I to know what was to happen?*

In the early morning hours of May 3rd, Mark woke me from my sleep to say good-bye. It was around five o'clock when he leaned over me, while I lay in bed, to awake me with a simple "I love you." His face brushed against mine as he kissed me and told me that he had stayed up late the night before to book airplane tickets for us to Turkey and Greece. I can still see the handsome smile spread across his face. He had purchased the tickets because my parents had invited us to go to Turkey with them to visit a friend of my father's side of the family. Mark and I were never ones to pass up traveling opportunities, and so we said we would go. We also decided to add a few days in Greece on our own at the end of the trip. We thought it might be our last chance to go on a big trip before having a baby. As Mark said his farewell that morning, he told me to book the nicest hotel in Greece. He said he wanted it to be special. And with that, he kissed me, flashed his million-dollar smile, and walked out of the bedroom, out of the house, and ultimately out of my life here on earth. That was the last time I saw my husband, my best friend, and the source of so much of my happiness.

After Mark left, I stayed in bed for another half hour, until I got up to get ready and then headed to work as usual. I remember that day as being a somewhat emotional day. It was one of those days when, for no particular reason, I just couldn't snap out of the peculiar uninvited melancholy that had overtaken my mood. Everyone around me seemed to be in a bit of a bad mood as well. Nothing too unusual with the day. Just an overall less-than-mediocre day—one of those unexplainable things.

After work I had to stay for a meeting with a group of staff members. My phone was off, as it always was throughout the day because of my teaching. The meeting went until around four o'clock, and after it was over I packed up my things to go home. I had decided in one of those mind-wandering moments during the meeting that I was going to stop by the store on my way home from work to purchase chips and guacamole. I had invited some coworkers over for Friday night, and I wanted to prepare for them. I grabbed my things, walked out of the building, and turned on my cell phone. I had five messages. I listened to the first one, and it was my mother-in-law, Vicky. She simply said to call her. The second message was from her, as was the third, and the fifth. In each message she said that she was in the area where I lived, and that I should call her. With each message, her voice grew more persistent as she continued to ask where I was. The thought crossed my mind that something was wrong. I shoved it aside and thought, "No, she's just being persistent as she sometimes can be." My stomach dropped when I realized that not one message was from Mark. I clearly remember stopping in the middle of the parking lot after listening to all the messages and realizing that not one was from him. I had told Mark to call me when the plane landed in Montana to let me know that he made it safely. I got into my car and immediately called his cell phone.

It went straight to voice mail. Nausea shot up from deep within me, but I was able to soothe it as I reminded myself that often when we were away from one another, we would call at night, after the day's activities were over. So, I proceeded to leave him a message to call me, and then I called Vicky back. She answered immediately and said that they were in Glen Ellyn and wanted to know when I was going to be back so we could grab a cup of coffee. I remember thinking that "they" probably meant her and Kim (a friend of the family). I also remember thinking that it was strange for her to just stop by unannounced, as she had never done that before. I decided I would put off my grocery shopping until after we had coffee. The sinking feeling of something being wrong entered my mind again, but I swiftly suppressed it.

After my forty-five-minute drive home from work, I pulled into the driveway and saw not only Vicky's car but also my father-in-law John's and my brother-in-law Mike's cars as well. Panic sprang up within my soul. I pushed it aside and forced a smile on my face as I grabbed my book bag and walked toward my back stairs. The back door of my home soon opened, and Bristol, my dog, came running out to meet me. I bent down to embrace her as I heard someone say in a surprisingly harsh tone of voice, "Bristol, no! Come here!" I raised my eyes to see John, Vicky, and Mike coming out of my home. Vicky was in front, and she moved toward me with her arms open wide. I don't remember the exact words that were said to me, but I think it was something like, "We lost Mark." Right then and there I collapsed on the deck floor, and I felt their hands upon me. I cried out continuously, "Are you sure? Are you sure?" and I remember Vicky saying, "Why would we lie about this?" I think I must have repeated the phrases "Are you sure?" and "No! No! No! It can't be!" over and over for hours. Eventually John said, "Let's get her inside." They all helped me in the door to my house and they led me to the living-room couch. We all sat there. We sat there for hours. A horrible silence filled the room and took up any space for words, conversations, and thoughts. I am unable to recall my in-laws' faces that day, all except for Vicky's face when she told me that my husband, her son, was dead.

Time is a difficult thing to measure. It is measured in seconds, minutes, hours, days, and so on. However, in the initial moments of tragedy, it feels as though time ceases to be measurable. It feels as though it stops altogether, and yet, somehow, minutes, hours, and days continue to go by. What once seemed like a twenty-four-hour period of time no longer feels the same. I don't remember the passing of time that afternoon when I found out Mark had died in a plane crash. I simply remember John, Vicky, Mike, and I sitting in the suffocating silence of my living room. We sat there staring quietly at the ceiling as the clock kept ticking, but all our hearts had stopped beating.

Eventually, Coffee, a minister friend of the family, appeared at the house. He quietly entered the room to join us in our silence. He asked me if I had called my parents to tell them the news of Mark's death, and I told him that I didn't want to have to call anyone and voice the words out loud. I responded that way because I feared that if I spoke the words *Mark died* out loud, the words would make it reality. I didn't want this to be my reality, and I was fighting it. However, in time I called my family, but I was unable to reach them right away. Eventually I was able to connect with my sister Kim. I remember having enough coherence to ask her if she was driving, and when she said no, I told her that Mark was dead. I voiced those horrible words out loud. I'm unsure of the exact words I used, but I am positive that I wasn't able to get all the words out clearly before I broke down sobbing. It still sends chills down my body to think of the sounds of horror that came from the other end of the phone when I told her. I hated that call. I hated having to voice the words that conveyed that my husband was dead and how it brought about the realization of that reality. I made only a few more calls: one to my friend Heather, one to my friend Amy, one to my friend Paige, and another to a coworker. Other than a few minor things, I don't remember much of those calls, as the details elude me. I was on autopilot at that point and operating in a complete state of shock.

At the time of Mark's death, I was living in Illinois, and my family lived in Minnesota. They were able to get plane tickets immediately and flew to me that very evening. The time between telling my sister the news of Mark's death and my family arriving at my house is a segment of existence that is lost to me. I do remember when they arrived at my house and I opened the door to find them huddled together, silent except for the sound of their tears. We embraced there on my doorstep, and our bodies shook in pain together. Eventually we let go of one another, and they slowly entered the house. I watched them approach the Wauterleks, tears running down their faces. My father swore, which he never does, as he paced the room until he finally joined the rest of us in the silence of our pain and defeat. The intensity of the shock I was experiencing seemed to absorb my tears. Ben, a good friend of ours, called. Upon hearing my voice, he broke down sobbing for what seemed like forever. I listened to him wail and wail and wail. My body stiffened, and I could not cry. I felt nothing at that point. Nothing. There were no more tears. At least not for a while. John asked if we should get something to eat. Everyone responded by saying that they were not hungry. And so, after hours of silence and stillness, the Wauterleks left my house to drive back to theirs.

That night I fell asleep with both of my sisters in my bed. I didn't sleep well because I was anxious for morning. Anxious to awake from this nightmare and find Mark in bed beside me where he belonged.

May 4, 2007

When morning came, I didn't look at my sisters beside me. I wanted it all to be but a nightmare that I had awaken from, and I didn't want to see any physical proof that it was, in fact, reality. I quietly slid out of bed, picked up the phone on the nightstand, and called Mark's cell phone while praying for him to answer. The call went immediately to voice mail, and the pain in the depths of my soul at that point was unbearable. I stumbled down the stairs to the living room and saw my mom reading her Bible on our couch. When I laid eyes on her, my body went limp. Sobbing, I collapsed into her arms. My father entered the room, and I felt his hands on my back, and then my sisters surrounded me as well. I'm not sure what I looked like in that moment, but it had to have been awful, truly awful. My body was tormented with pain, and as I sobbed, I raised my fists in the air and cried out, "No, no, no!" The tears came from so far deep within, it tore me apart to get them out. The grief physically ravaged me.

The days following, I lived in a completely incoherent state of mind. I remember only very small fragments of time. At some point the next day, our closest friends from Minnesota, Matt and Heather, arrived at the house. I can remember them coming to the back door, as they had always done when they visited, and I met them there. We embraced, and the three of us cried as we clung to one another in our grief. Later, my family drove me to the Wauterlek's home, about forty-five minutes away. There were many people there, and yet only silence was experienced—the same awful, horrible silence that appeared to follow me wherever I went. On occasion, whispers and sobbing could be heard. I did my best to talk with those who were there, but eventually I wanted, and needed, to be alone. I had my sister Anna and my best friend Heather come upstairs with me to one of the bedrooms. We crawled into bed, and I asked Anna to crawl behind me and hold me as Mark would. I wanted to close my eyes, feel her arms around me, and pretend that they were Mark's. She did so without so much as a word, and soon my body shook in pain as the tears poured out. I was wailing (and I use the word *wailing* because *crying* does not come close to describing the magnitude and intensity of the tears). There are, in fact, no words to accurately describe the grief. My body writhed in pain and contorted in every physical effort to soothe itself. It was truly unbearable. I was so engulfed in grief that I would lose awareness of my surroundings and eventually enter a state of numbness.

Shock is a thief. It steals reality from us as well as entire passages of time. However, it ironically acts as our protector. It keeps us from feeling the full magnitude of the sorrow. It allows it in, but only in manageable pieces. Piece by piece we eventually feel all the sorrow but still have lost passages of time. Shock simply won't let us feel the reality and the intensity of all the many losses that the one loss fully represents. *Shock* is perhaps the best word to describe my feelings in the days after Mark's death. I am able to recall only fragments of my life at that time. For that I am grateful. I don't want to remember those days.

Mark's Funeral: Week of May 6

Mark and I had moved to Illinois from Minnesota two years into our marriage and four years before his death. We had many good friends from our time in Minnesota, and they all came in for the funeral. I clearly remember sitting on my front doorstep a few days after his death with my cousin's wife, my best friend from growing up, and my two sisters as we painted our toenails (seems so strange now to think that I was painting my toenails). Most of what I remember is just moments of intense grief. However, a person cannot live in that intensity for extended periods of time. The body won't allow it, and so we do things to try to occupy time and numb the mind—"normal" things like painting toenails. As we painted our nails that sunny afternoon, a caravan of cars filled with friends from Minnesota pulled into the driveway. I hadn't seen these dear friends in months and, like Pavlov's dogs, I automatically responded to the sight of them with excitement. I had only happy memories with these people, and therefore it was natural to feel excitement upon seeing them. As my friends piled out of their cars, tears spilled from their eyes when they caught sight of me. I embraced them all, and yet I could not cry. Their bodies shook with pain, and I struggled to make sense of it all. I had already cried more than I had in my entire life. I was numb and at a loss for what had become of me.

During those days, I remember going out to eat a lot, yet I don't remember the act of eating. I remember being surrounded by friends, yet I don't remember the specifics of what we talked about or how we passed the time. I am able to recall so little of the week between Mark's death and his funeral. Unfortunately, one thing that I do remember is when I went to the funeral home. I made it through most of the planning and only left when it came time to pick out the casket. My parents and the Wauterleks kept giving me opportunities to get out of planning anything. They were guardians of my well-being, but I felt the need to get through it all. I felt the responsibility to push myself. As we were making arrangements with the funeral director, a good friend of the Wauterleks (a woman probably in her late sixties or early seventies) showed up at the funeral home to give us her condolences. She had lost her husband three years prior. As she embraced me, I noticed that I felt relatively little. I was shut off emotionally at that point. However, many hours later I was looking out the window of the car as we were driving, and from seemingly out of nowhere, I burst into tears. I had thought of this family friend, this widow, and through my tears I cried out, "She has so many less years to live without her husband! I have too many! I am too young!" I stared out the window, tears streaming down my face. Looking back, it still makes me cry to think of that moment. The terror of realizing that I could possibly live fifty more years on this earth without him was incredibly overwhelming. I can easily go back to that moment and feel the pain I felt then. I can feel the despair. I can feel the nausea. I wanted to be with Mark. Never before had I wished to be older so that I could die sooner. This is certainly no way to live. I can't imagine what my parents felt watching their daughter in such pain and being able to do nothing about it.

Mark's funeral was—and is—a blur. I have flashbacks from time to time, as my mind attempts to take in more of it in an effort to process it all. There were a couple thousand people at the visitation, and I embraced all who waited in line. I was told how strong I was, but it wasn't my strength getting me through: it was the strength I received from Christ, along with a healthy dose of shock. I had focused my mind on planning the funeral and getting tasks accomplished. It wasn't until the burial at the cemetery that I finally lost it in front of everyone. I remember that the family was brought to the casket and led to put our hands on it. I didn't want to. Everything within me fought this. As I reluctantly touched the casket with my visibly shaking hand, my mind was overcome with the fact that this casket held the remains of my husband. It was too much to bear! Pain erupted within my soul, and I released a downpour of tears. I was soon led away from the casket and embraced by my father. I'm sure he was crying, but I have no recollection of his face—or of anyone's face for that matter. The sheer weight of the pain caused my legs to collapse, and my father held me up. Someone else then led me to the car, although I can't remember who. It's strange now to think how much I was led around in those days.

Week after the Funeral

My family stayed with me for a week or so after the funeral, until eventually they had to leave to return to their work, their homes, and their lives. My mom and my friend Heather stayed behind with me for another week. I remember my dad, my sisters, Heather's husband Matt, and their son Isaiah pulling out of the driveway for their ride home. They looked miserable leaving me. I could see it on their faces, and I felt lost in the confusion of what to do with myself. After they pulled out of the driveway, my mom suggested going to the mall so that she could get a birthday present for my dad. And so I drove the three of us in silence. I had no interest in shopping and I, like a zombie, moved one foot in front of the other as I followed my mom around the mall, while Heather followed me. I was confused as to why my mom was buying a present at all. Didn't she know that material items were so meaningless now? Perhaps she just needed an activity to keep her mind and body busy. Normally I would have felt that I needed to buy him a gift too. However, there was nothing normal about me anymore, and I certainly wasn't able to comprehend the purpose in purchasing anything. I believe Heather felt much the same as I did. As my mom started to go into the first store on her list, I told her that I didn't feel like joining her, and that I would wait on the bench outside. Heather stayed with me, and as we sat together silently in our collective grief, I saw for the first time all the strangers before me who were living life so completely differently from how I was feeling inside. I first noticed those that were smiling, laughing, holding hands, and carrying bags filled with things that most likely gave them a fleeting moment of happiness upon being purchased. A panic rose up from deep within, and although I tried to barricade my tear ducts with sheer will power, I failed to keep the tears at bay. The dam broke. It was the first time I saw people living life, completely unaffected by the loss of Mark. It frightened me to see that life was going on all around me when I had died along with my husband just days before. I was the walking dead in the land of the living. I turned to Heather and discovered she had just experienced the same feeling. We were both so taken back by seeing people going about "normal" life. As my mom came out of the store, I told her we had to leave. I did my best to avoid a complete mental breakdown as we hurriedly walked to the car. I drove us back to my house with shaky feet and a feeble mind. Just as soon as I got out of the car and walked up the back steps of my house, I released all the pain that had been building. I completely and truly lost it. Heather sat with me there and we cried for hours, literally hours. There were no words, just pain in the form of tears and silence. The tears came unceasingly until a small amount of relief was met. I wondered, honestly and truly, how I was going to live. Not only live as in the idea of wondering how to live life without Mark, but live as in being able to breathe. I didn't know if it was possible at that point.

Eventually a week went by. A long, pain-filled week with nothing productive to show for it. Heather and my mom needed to get home to Minnesota, and so I went with them. I remember the panic I felt about leaving, and I tried to postpone the trip. It made me anxious and worried to think about leaving my house. In examining these feelings, I realized that it was because I thought that maybe Mark would be coming back home. Maybe he wasn't truly gone after all, and I wanted to greet him when he walked through the door. Logically, I knew he wasn't coming home. However, my emotions and logic didn't always align. All I knew was that my heart ached for him and I couldn't bear to miss him if he were to return. I didn't share what I was feeling with Heather and my mom, because I knew my thoughts were illogical. I felt the need to push through the unrealistic emotions, and so I reluctantly left with them for Minnesota. I felt panic from the very moment when we left and throughout the entire time I was there. I hated the trip. I hated being away from our house in Illinois, and I hated that my childhood home in Minnesota could not bring me any comfort, any relief from the reality of

Mark's death. What happened to the happy childhood I once had? Where was my relief from the pain?

I felt as though I was living a life to which seemingly no one could relate: a life of loneliness and sorrow; a life that was once ideal, until it became defined by death; a life for which words cannot begin to adequately convey the thoughts and feelings that daily go through my mind. My mind is so difficult to control. A life of extremes defines me now. *Widow:* the word defines me now. It defines my life.

May 23, 2007

I went out and purchased a body pillow within the first month after Mark died. I had been told it would help me sleep. I would pull it up next to my body at night, and it provided me with some small sense of comfort. And yet, it didn't do enough. Not nearly enough. These feeble attempts of mine continue to disappoint me every time I reach over and hope to feel Mark. The body pillow does nothing to keep me from loneliness, just as the presence of others has not kept me from feeling lonely. Loneliness is such a strange thing. I've been surrounded by many who love and care for me, and yet I feel lonely—a deep, aching loneliness that takes over and suffocates the whole of me. I beg for relief from it, and though I try to fight it off with the company of friends, I cannot control it. There is no escaping it. It creeps in and suffocates. I endure with the hope of knowing that eventually it will leave and grant me some reprieve from the pain, even if only for a short time. I know that although it will leave, it will also come back. It always comes back to take control of me once again. Over and over it comes and goes.

May 24, 2007

I don't seem to feel much these days, other than constant, lingering, dull pain. It seems as though I live the same day over and over again as I await the awakening from this nightmare. The days seem the same, even though the locations and people change. I try to make some plans for the future but find myself numb and unable to make decisions. Even the most minor decisions, such as what to eat, can be too difficult for me. Everything is seemingly futile, and I find myself waiting for the Rapture. I cannot go on like this, living this way, and so I believe the Rapture must come soon. I want to move forward; I just can't seem to do so. Perhaps that is why with each new place I go (my parents' cabin or Minnesota, for example), I feel such pain upon arriving. It is the painful realization that my grief is impossible to escape. It follows me wherever I go, and it robs me of any joy.

Going out to eat, something that I used to enjoy immensely, is meaningless to me now. I put on my best face and go through the old motions of dressing up in a futile effort to regain the happiness I once experienced from the event. My efforts are rendered useless as I become painfully aware of how it seems as though everyone else in the restaurant gets to laugh and enjoy their meal without painful memories haunting them.

Grief appears random and unceasing in its pursuit of me. There is no formula for controlling it, as I don't know what will set it off or when it will hit. What I do know is that it will visit me time and time again to take control and weaken me from the inside. How do I move on from this? How do I heal? Grief, leave me alone. I beg you, please.

Since Mark's death, people have asked me if I am afraid to fly. My response is, "I'm afraid to live." It terrifies me so much more to think of living a long life without him than to think of dying anytime soon. Dangerous situations on earth don't scare me.

People have been around me constantly. It's been a source of great comfort and distraction, but it is also incredibly difficult. Everything is this way for me now. A conflict. A paradox. A contradiction dripping with irony. I desire the company of people and yet wish to be left alone. I want to be blanketed in conversational noise and yet covet the peace of silence. The condolences of those around me fail to comfort, and their efforts seem useless. As for the comfort found in faith, I know that I should be reading the Bible. I crave it, know I need it, and yet haven't picked it up more than once. *I am paralyzed!* Paralyzed from feeling much, doing much, and being much. My emotions are all over the place and unpredictable. I fear what truly thinking about the implications of Mark's death will do to me. I'm already disabled in so many ways. Will it kill me altogether? Spiral me even lower into the depths of despair? Is that even possible?

Thoughts that I've had today about the future
1. I'm afraid to live alone but also feel as though I need to take the challenge.
2. I feel some excitement and certainly a strong desire to work with needy children. I'm afraid to quit teaching, but think I must not continue at my same job. I need to have the most good as possible come from this in order to survive. This seems to imply a job change. I believe I should work with children from low-income neighborhoods instead of the upper middle-class children I have been teaching.
3. I will travel. I've always greatly enjoyed traveling.
4. I will substitute teach and volunteer in order to scope out possibilities for a future career move.
5. I would like to live with my sister in downtown Chicago. It could be fun someday, even though it is hard to imagine that now. I used to wish that Mark and I could have lived in the city.

May 25, 2007

I drove up north to my parents' cabin with Matt, Heather, and their son the other night. In the morning, we went into the town to get groceries, and while at the store, I decided to purchase a notebook in which to write my thoughts and feelings about life. Perhaps I was inspired by C. S. Lewis's book *A Grief Observed* (although *inspired* seems too positive a word to describe my feelings these days).

I am absolutely terrified of what life will be like without Mark. I understand that I can go on and perhaps even experience happiness again in my life. There is possibility for that, and logic tells me so. The pain of losing Mark will probably lessen with time (or so "they" say), but what I can't believe is that my life will ever be as enjoyable. I'm afraid the pain is too much. It has robbed me of the joy for living.

I am alone, and I don't like being alone. However, I don't want to be with anyone but Mark. I feel as though no man could ever live up to him in my eyes. Period. The life that I so enjoyed, the life I lived with him, is gone. My dreams of having a family with a wonderful husband were buried along with him on May 3rd. *Oh Lord, I don't know what to do! I understand that I am to turn to you and follow your will. I am just so confused as to what that looks like. Honestly, I don't really want to, either. Lord, I have to admit that I don't much care for your will if it involved taking Mark from me. I want Mark back! I want my life with him! I want the life I once had that was so full of dreams, happiness, and fulfillment.*

I knew that with Mark, life was almost too good. So many people appeared to have struggles that we just didn't have. It made me feel that we were about due for something bad to happen. I guess I just thought that the something bad would be more along the lines of being infertile or losing a job. However, I didn't necessarily even believe that any of those things would really happen. My life with Mark was comprised of almost everything that the world had to offer. He loved me, and I loved, trusted, and respected him. We had the world before us—or so it seemed.

Looking back, I can say that I was aware that my love for him was possibly a hindrance to serving the Lord. It was so easy to get caught up in arranging trips together, planning for a family, decorating our house, and desiring other things of the world. I did fear at times that these things would distract me from seeing the Lord's will for my life. I always felt that there was a calling from him that I hadn't tapped into yet. I just didn't imagine that it would ever be without Mark. How do I discern God's will for my life now when I can't even decide the little things like what to eat? How do I look for and listen to God when I am so completely dead to the world and even to myself? I don't want to enter into any new life without Mark. It will be too evident that he is missing. I ask not only how do I go on without him but also how does the world as a whole go on without him? Don't people know the magnitude of who they lost? Shouldn't a tragedy as tremendous as this have such an enormous impact that it leaves me in the position to live with increased passion for God? It seems I *have* to live for God now, because there is nothing else. I know this, because I certainly can't live for myself. What else could I live for? I'm broken and searching for the Great Physician to heal me. I must live for God and for others. It's the only choice that I have, as living for only me will not heal. What does this mean, though?

I feel sick all the time. I am sick when left alone in my thoughts and sick when surrounded by others in conversation. Many times when I am in the middle of a conversation completely unrelated to Mark, I find that I can't stop thinking of him and his death. The physical pain feels permanently intrusive. I want to fast-forward to the point where I won't feel this intense permeating pain anymore. Is there a calendar on which I can cross out the dates on a countdown to recovery? How long will it take? The pain is so intense! I've been told that it will never completely go away, but I want and need it to lessen. It has to lessen soon.

Dear Jesus, please talk to me directly and passionately. My ears are attentive, and my heart is waiting. Please, Lord, please! I am on my knees, without an ounce of strength left within me. I rely solely on you. Don't let me fall deeper than I already have. I don't want to live a bitter, meaningless, self-absorbed life. Tell me what to do and I'll do it. I'll work harder than anyone else.

Ideas and Goals
1. Write a grief book
2. Finish graduate school
3. Run a marathon
4. Join a widow support group
5. Move to the city
6. Write a children's book
7. Find a volunteer opportunity

May 26, 2007

It is morning now, and I find that mornings are slightly easier to take than the darkness that night brings. My soul is heavy in the blackness of evening, and the ache that it feels eases away with the freshness of light that the early hours bring. The morning brings the sunshine of awareness that I have made it through another day. And with each passing day, there is hope that I will survive this, that perhaps there will be meaning for me again.

Today I remembered a time in the recent past when I had thought of the possibility of Mark dying. It was a very brief thought, and it was so incredibly painful that I suppressed it immediately. I wondered where this thought had come from. In the past, my mind had allowed in the thoughts of various potential tragedies for brief moments: thoughts of war in America, becoming afflicted with cancer or some other horrible disease, and losing all our money or possessions. All these thoughts produced a panic deep within that is uncomfortable to bear, and so I often pushed them aside. However, when I thought of losing Mark, that one singular thought was the worst of them all. I believed that if that were to ever happen, I wouldn't be able to continue to live. So, although Mark's death came as a shock, I can't say in all honesty that I hadn't thought of it before. When I try to think back on any thoughts that I had had about the possibility of Mark dying before me, two particular thoughts come to mind. I don't remember exactly where and when I had them; I just remember them.

First, I remember thinking about our elderly years and that I didn't want him to die before I did. I thought it would be way too painful and horrible to be left behind, alone, without him. However, I also loved him too much to truly want to die first and leave him in that kind of pain. Therefore, I had hoped that we would die together, preferably in our old age or at least perhaps on our way back from some fantastic vacation together. God never made a deal with me on these terms, yet I can't help but feel the disappointment and confusion as if he had.

Although the first thought of Mark's death was a more prominent possibility in my mind, I do remember one time (most likely this was triggered by some movie or book) when I wondered if I would prefer his dying if we were young and without kids. It is so strange to remember this now. It unnerves me. *Lord, were you preparing me on some level for what was to come?* Strange what the mind remembers, and stranger still that I can look back and think about those thoughts that I had before the tragedy of losing Mark. One certainly cannot prepare for this. One cannot mentally prepare for death. My mind has been aware, at least on an intellectual level, that death can come like a thief in the night to anyone anywhere. However, intellect and logic did not prepare me for when it happened, especially at such a young age and especially when I loved him more than anything else in the world.

I wish that we had children. For so many reasons, I wish that we had them. If we had a child, I would have a living, breathing piece of him, a piece of his flesh and blood. I also would not have to feel the loneliness and resentment of growing old without a family of my own. I wouldn't have to feel the pressure that I imagine I will feel someday to get married and have children. I'm terrified that I might make a mistake and remarry just to have children and a family.

Lord, please be with me (as I know you are). I don't expect that you will take all the pain away, as that seems completely impossible. But I do expect and trust that you'll give me your comfort and peace in the midst of it, for this is your promise. Please make yourself known to me in more ways than ever before, and may I learn how to discern your will in a clear way. Lord, tell me what to do today and in every day that follows. What should my plans and dreams look like now that the ones I had for myself are shattered? I'm willing to follow you more now than ever before. Scrape me up off this floor, strengthen me, and lead me forward. I am willing.

Thoughts that I have had today about the future
1. Honestly, not many. I've tried to avoid thinking about any day beyond today. Today is difficult enough.
2. I am finding it impossible to even entertain the thought of going back to teaching this year. I don't want people to

examine my every move, and I don't want to be a source of sadness and pity.

I am feeling so conflicted—all the time conflicted! Tonight I went to a family friend's cabin with my parents. I didn't really feel like going, as I hate thinking about how people will react to me and how I should respond. I often feel the burden of comforting others and making sure that they don't feel uncomfortable around me. However, I don't really want to be alone either.

I hadn't seen these family friends since the funeral. When we got to their place, they hugged me and quickly went on with the dinner "as usual." There were a couple of times when Mark's name was mentioned, but he was referred to in a manner that didn't suggest his death. References to him were short, sporadic, and few. When I look back, I can remember only Mark's good friend and myself saying Mark's name that evening. Although I didn't necessarily want to talk about Mark or his death, I also couldn't stand having a dinner where his name was barely mentioned. It bothered me. It also bothered me that I seemed to be ignored on some small level. Perhaps this was only in my mind, but it felt as though Mark's death—and my condition—was the elephant in the room. It felt as though no one really looked at me or asked me any questions. I was avoided, and that upset me. I realize that this, on some level, was incredibly hypocritical because I often avoid discussions, and I can't mention Mark's name in past tense or use the words *death* or *died* either. When talking about what happened, I have noticed that we all use the word *accident* and avoid any of the "d" words. I took a sleeping pill that night.

May 27, 2007

I woke up at ten in the morning and continued to lie in bed with my dog, Bristol, for some time. *I can't do this anymore!* I don't want to, and I don't know how to cure myself from the sickness that plagues me continuously. How can this be true? *Lord, how can this be true? Where is Mark?*

I've been trying to stay strong for others and, truthfully, for myself as well. I am fearful of letting the reality of it all sink in. I try to engage in "normal" activities, but I often only stare off into space. Even if I am able to maintain eye contact and appear to be engaged in an activity, my mind is impossibly elusive and unable to be tamed. I have pretended to watch various movies with friends or family members only to think about Mark or why anything matters through the entire film.

When I do linger on thoughts of my new reality, I find that, surprisingly, I don't always cry anymore. Perhaps it is because it just doesn't seem real. Certainly someday the reality of his death and all its horrible implications for my life will feel very real. *How long, Lord? When?*

Vicky called me yesterday and cried to me on the phone for a long time. I sat in the bedroom, listened to her, and somehow felt numb to it. I don't understand it. Why is she crying? I don't know how to make it feel real to me, I don't know if I want it to, and I certainly don't want to move on to a life without Mark.

I try my best to feel excited about all the possibilities for my future, but I find that even if I feel a small amount of excitement, it lasts for a mere second and is trailed by intense sadness. Some things have brought fleeting moments of excitement to me: thoughts of living in the city (although this scares me too), ministry volunteer opportunities, and traveling. Unfortunately there is so much more that terrifies me: living alone, growing old alone, having to be solely responsible for the finances, selling the house, being taken advantage of, being avoided, feeling this utter despair and sadness the rest of my life, and the constant ache of missing Mark! *Lord, please take these fears from me.* I read James this morning, and later, Job. They gave me comfort, if even on a small level.

May 28, 2007

I woke up a little earlier than normal today at quarter to nine in the morning. My waking thoughts continue to be twofold: (1)

"This can't be real!" and (2), "Do I really have to go through another day like this?" Every day I awake with this terrible reality.

It is a beautiful, sunny day, and I long to be able to drink it in and savor it completely. I long for the simple pleasures such as enjoying the gift of ideal weather. However, my ability to enjoy beauty was taken from me when Mark died. I want to forget my reality, but I cannot. I try and try but continually fail. It is impossible to enjoy anything when I feel this ravaged by grief. My grief is like cancer in my stomach. The intensity of the pain it causes subsides a little over time; yet it never completely disappears. The pain is there. Always there. Making me sick time and time again. There is no medicine to cure this pain; even time cannot heal me completely, it seems.

June 2, 2007

It has been five days since I last wrote in this journal. Since then, I came back to Illinois from my parents' cabin with Heather and her son, Isaiah. I find that I want to be in my home. It is comforting for now, even though I think that eventually I will want to move because living in the suburbs as a young, single woman doesn't sound very enticing. Also, the cost of maintaining the home is too much. I can understand why "they" say to wait a year before making any big changes (I'd really like to meet them by the way, whoever "they" are). I don't know of anywhere else I would live right now.

I woke up this morning and read some more of the book of Job in the Bible. It confused me to no end. Is God testing me? Did he plan for the plane to crash? I cannot get past knowing that he at least allowed it. But did he plan for it? That is different to me. I don't understand, and I know I never will, at least not here on earth. It is too difficult to believe that God made the crash happen, although I am faced with the reality that it is a possibility. If God loves me, why would he hurt me like this? All my past theological discussions about the problem of suffering are far too real now.

And so I run. I run a lot. It helps me to deal with the stress and sadness that I feel. Anger is my fuel. I am constantly anxious. I cannot sit still, and yet I find that the weariness of the grief weighs me down, rendering me useless for the responsibilities of life. Paying bills and organizing Mark's things are both too difficult. I cannot think clearly. I find myself wondering when Mark is going to come home, and the anxiousness inside grows and takes over the whole of me. Running helps to clear my mind and let out some of my anger.

I cannot grasp the reality of Mark's death; and to be honest, I don't want to. Part of me is afraid to let it sink in. I am afraid of experiencing pain worse than that which I already feel. How is it even possible for one to live through the crushing blow of life's hardest hit—death? I haven't cried much lately. Some quiet, small tears have been shed, but no sobbing or wailing. Perhaps I am holding it in, and perhaps it can't be released because I don't allow myself to feel the fullness of my sadness. I'm afraid to be alone for any extended period of time, because I think the immense pain will reveal itself in full measure then. I'm so grateful for having been surrounded by people. *Lord, thank you for my friends and family.* They are an amazing blessing, and they help to ease at least some portion of my loneliness. I have friends staying with me through June, and my feelings about it are contradictory. I am grateful that my friends are stay-at-home moms who have the ability to stay with me, and yet I'm resentful that my friends are mothers and have families of their own. *Lord, I wanted that too, and so I want to be left alone on some level as a result. I want to be alone, and yet I fear it. The anxiety is overwhelming. Lord, make these people go away so that Mark can come back to me!* I have yet to spend that first night alone, and the thought of it terrifies me. I'm so confused, because everything is in constant discord.

Mark's cousins, who are our age, are having a party tonight. I want to go because I enjoy them, I love parties, and I want to do something "normal." However, I'm terrified. I worry about how people will treat me and how I will ultimately feel as a result. I don't know how I'll feel once I'm there. I used to be such an emotionally controlled person. Now, I don't know who I am. I am a mess, and I despise not being able to know how things will affect me. Everything is this way now. Honestly, I don't want to do anything without Mark, and this, unfortunately, makes it nearly impossible for me to make decisions.

My coworker stopped by yesterday and said that our principal had told her that she was going to offer me a year off. I think this sounds like a good idea; however, I don't know—even when I feel relatively confident about a decision and say what I want, I question it. Nothing seems right. I just want Mark. I want to go and be with him. How can someone, as the Bible says, be made one with someone else and then be ripped apart from that person? Half of me is gone—the better half. I don't know how this works without him. How do I function as half? How do I function as an amputee? I am missing such a large part of who I am. *Please, Lord, help me. Give me strength. Show me what to do.*

June 3, 2007

My friend Heather who has been staying with me, her son Isaiah, and I went to church with John and Vicky today. We decided to attend the church of one of the ministers who spoke at Mark's funeral. He is a wonderful man, and he leads a growing church in the city. As we parked and made our way to the church doors, John picked up Isaiah and carried him. Heather and I followed behind and watched the two of them together. John has always been wonderful with children, and he had expressed to Mark and me that we should have many of our own: "The world needs good Christian people like you to raise healthy, strong children. Our society would benefit." These words rang in my ears as I watched him carry a child in his arms. That should be my son! That should be his grandchild that he is holding! *Why, Lord, why don't I have a child? Why doesn't John have a grandson of his own?* My heart ached for both of us. The world makes no sense to me. He would be an amazing grandfather, and it seems incredibly unfair that he wasn't given any grandchildren. On some small level, I feel like a failure. I feel like I let him down. I should have given him a grandchild. I would do anything to have given him a grandchild. Perhaps it would have helped to ease some of the pain of losing Mark for both of us.

June 4, 2007

I dropped Heather and Isaiah off at the airport this morning. She had stayed with me for about a month, and it was difficult to watch her go. We both shed tears. Yet, as I pulled away from the airport, a sense of relief washed over me. I was finally ready to be alone. I was both needing and craving it. On some level, I believe I felt that way because when a friend would leave, it felt as though Mark must be coming home. That was the way it had always been before. If he was on a hunting or fishing trip, I would often have a friend visit. It just doesn't seem real that I am truly going to be alone. It doesn't seem real that he is not coming home.

I went to work today to visit my second-grade classroom for the first time since May 3. Today was the last full day of school for the year. I felt so many emotions. I was scared and anxious about what to expect. Anxiety continues to be a common emotion for me. It always lingers around, as if it is one of my closest companions. Confusion is always close by as well. I was feeling confused about how to act around others. I live in the awareness that many are watching and analyzing me. Confusion leads to anxiousness. I said a prayer, gathered whatever small amount of courage I had, and walked into my classroom with a smile on my face. The kids were excited to see me. They told me about what they had been doing since I left, and then they performed their fairy-tale plays for me. It felt good to see them, and yet it seemed I was experiencing them through a thick haze. When the school day was over, and I was exhausted, my coworkers whisked me away to another room where parents wouldn't know to look for me. They didn't want me to be overwhelmed by parents. My coworkers were very kind and thoughtful. We spent time talking, and I hid from them the intensity of how I really felt. I knew they were analyzing me, and I did my best to look and act strong. Afterward, a few of my close coworker friends and I went out for dinner and then came back to my house for ice cream. One of my coworkers presented me with a gift from the staff. I was confused. Why was I receiving a gift for Mark's death? I didn't want to open the present. Beautifully wrapped gifts are supposed to represent happy times like birthdays and holidays. They are not for tragedies. It made me feel uncomfortable to open it, but I hid my true emotions behind a smile, so as to avoid making anyone upset. I knew that they were trying to do what they could to help, and I appreciated that.

Later in the evening, Ben (a close friend of ours who was in town for business) came over. We went to dinner together and talked about Mark and about life. We walked back home from dinner with our arms around each other. He spent the night in our guest room, and I remember wondering what my neighbors thought about seeing a young man staying the night at our home. I remember, too, that after some time thinking about it, I didn't care. They don't know what a good friend he has been to Mark and me. They don't know what it is like to be me now.

It was my first night alone in the bed that Mark and I had shared. I crawled in on my side of the bed and slept there without moving. Old habits are hard to break.

July 15, 2007

The Wauterleks and I had been invited to go to Spain with a pastor friend of the family. This pastor was on sabbatical, and he decided to visit Spain with his family, as he often does. He told us that it would probably be healing for us to get away and that he desired to minister to us there. John and Vicky generously offered to pay for my way and for a friend's way as well. Mike wasn't going to go, and they were thoughtful to recognize that I may want a friend along. I invited Heather, and she came with us.

We've been here for a total of eleven days. The trip has been both enjoyable and difficult at the same time. There have been moments of relief during times when Heather and I explored the city alone, and it felt as though we were twenty again, traveling Spain together as we had done nine years earlier. There were times of gratitude as well. John and Vicky have taken care of the entire trip. Their generosity continues to impress me. However, there have been struggles and conflict. It is hard to weather through the storm of grief as a collective group. We have all steered our ships differently when caught in this storm. Vicky has wanted to have intense discussions about faith, and I have had no interest in such discussions. I find it stressful to try to make my needs known while trying to meet some of her needs at the same time. She appears to feel the same about me, as I can sense the struggle from within her as well. I so desperately desire to avoid any heavy conversations. They make me so tired, and I am already exhausted. Why is it that Vicky seeks out intense conversations and I avoid them? Although we are both grieving deeply, our means of dealing with it are so different. The initial desire that I had to constantly be with the Wauterleks is beginning to wear off. I'm too tired to try to be for them what I cannot, and I'm too tired to challenge them when they seemingly treat me as though I were their teenage daughter. I want to make my needs known but also respect theirs. It has proven to be far more difficult than expected. They mean well, and I know that it comes from a desire to protect me, as most parents feel this way. They have told me that I am more than a daughter-in-law to them, that I am a daughter in their eyes. I feel the same connection to them and have referred to them as Mom and Dad. However, I am an adult, and it is strange for them to tell me that they don't want me to walk around Spain at night. They can't protect me in this way. Besides, protect me from what? I don't care if anything happens to me. Mark is gone. Nothing else matters much. I know that they want to protect me, but there is a struggle, as I am a grown woman. They are not the only ones to treat me this way; many others have exhibited overprotective behavior toward me. But I feed into it, because at times I want to go back to being a child, to being protected and taken care of. I am aware that I contradict myself in this.

I took off my wedding ring for the first time on the second day here. I looked down at my hand that day, and I hated seeing it there. It made me angry, and I wanted to throw it into the sea. My husband was dead, and I was no longer married. I couldn't deal with it. I thought perhaps taking it off and pretending as though I were back in time, when I was traveling around Spain in college, would help. It upset Vicky that I had taken off the ring, but she tried to understand. I didn't want to talk about it on the trip. I wanted to forget everything as best as I could. I wanted to pretend that I was twenty again, living in that time in my life when I was naive and the world was an exciting place, full of promises.

Although there are some struggles to be worked out, I know the Wauterleks and I will always be there for one another. Right now it is difficult, because we can't be what the other needs, and we are all hurting so much. There is too much pain. The wounds are too fresh.

As we get ready to leave Spain, my anxiousness grows again. I hate that I don't have Mark to come home to! I hate it! Thinking about going back literally makes me sick. My stomach churns and I feel nauseous. I don't want to go home, but I don't want to stay in Spain either. I'm neither here nor there. My heart is in heaven, where my husband now resides. With each moment that we get closer to going back to the United States, my heart races faster. What am I going to do now? How will I feel at home? I have decisions to make when I get back, and I don't know what to do. I have a meeting with my principal, and I have to tell her if I am going to take next year off. I'm leaning toward taking the year off, but I am worried, anxious, and confused about the decision. Nothing seems right. *God, I know that you are there, but please show yourself and your will to me. I need you, Lord. I need you now!*

August 4–11, 2007

My sister Anna and her close friend had planned a trip to Ireland, and they invited me to come with them. It was a great time, considering the circumstances. Many fun memories were made, even though there were tears sprinkled throughout. Just when we were having fun and I was thinking about what a nice escape it was, my grief would sneak up on me and steal away my sense of happiness. Perhaps the good news is that I am now able to laugh and have a good time, even though I continue to burst into tears at unknown moments.

One evening while in a picturesque town in Ireland, we went out for a nice dinner filled with wine, delicious food, and laughter. After dinner, as we were making our way back to the hotel, I could feel the volcano in my soul begin to tremble. The pressure eventually erupted in tears. I'm not certain of what in particular triggered it. It seems to do this, to build and build until the walls of my soul can no longer contain it. My sister and her friend cried with me in the hotel, and my sister embraced me as I mourned. Both of them had boyfriends at the time of the trip, and they did their best not to talk about them at length even though I had told them that they could. Their compassion was appreciated. Truthfully, I don't want to hear about boyfriends or husbands or babies. I try so desperately not to be selfish. I want to be happy for everyone, and I don't want to drown in a sea of my sorrow. I don't want the feelings of "poor me" to sweep me away and drown me in a pool of self-pity. It's so difficult—difficult, too, that my sister said that she had never met anyone like Mark. In her words, "there just aren't guys like him out there."

For our last night in Dublin, we decided to go out for a nice dinner and then to a pub down the street for drinks. Once we were in the pub, a large group of guys quickly approached us. They were celebrating the twenty-ninth birthday of their friend. They bought us drinks and asked us to join them in celebrating that evening. As we talked with them, two of the men showed interest in me. This was not a common experience for me over the past six years, as I had often been out only with Mark or with other married women. In all honesty, it felt good to have some interest shown in me. However, at the same time, it made me feel ill. My life has become a life of contradictions! One of the men asked me why I wasn't married, and I responded by saying that I hadn't found the right guy. I lied—I didn't want to talk about death and experience the awkwardness between us that would most likely ensue. After the words of my lie were spoken out loud, I instantly began to shake, and dizziness overcame me. I felt horrible. I couldn't lie to myself or anyone else. After a while, and after he continued to show romantic interest in me, I couldn't take it anymore. I told the guy the truth. I told him that my husband had died in a plane crash. He immediately apologized in a very sincere manner and gave me a hug. It felt better to tell the truth than to avoid it or mask it with a lie. I think that from this point on, I will speak the truth up front. My sister later told me that she knew I most likely would have started to cry if the guy at the pub had tried to kiss me or hold my hand, and that she was prepared to leave at any time if this was to happen. Luckily it didn't.

Coming back from Ireland was extremely difficult. I started to hyperventilate on the plane as the thought of having to go home to a life without Mark descended on me like the heaviness of night. What am I going home to? I want to continue to travel the world to escape it all. I would continue to run far away from home and never look back, if it were an option.

August 15, 2007

Tonight I had dinner with some college friends. One lives in the Chicago area, and the other two live in Minneapolis and had come to Chicago to visit and to celebrate a thirtieth birthday. We all met up at our friend's house in Evanston and then went from there to have dinner at a Spanish restaurant in the city. Although I hadn't kept in much contact with these friends over the years, it felt easy to be with them again. They were my "wild and fun" friends from college—the kind of friends with whom I could have a good time but rarely confided in. I knew that they would probably just want to have a celebratory night and that they wouldn't ask me too much, if at all, about how I was doing. I liked that. Conversation during dinner was light, except for when we talked about the marriage problems that one of them was experiencing. She had been involved in an affair, and her husband had recently found out. She had always been a very open person, and so I wasn't surprised that she was sharing this with me. I felt both anger and pain upon hearing the news. *Why, Lord? Why my marriage and not theirs? Why end something so good? We did what was right, didn't we?* I did my best to suppress these emotions and to just listen to her. My heart is so sensitive to the world's pain, and so sensitive to my own. It hurts.

Our deep conversation was abruptly ended when a pitcher of sangria was sent to our table by a group of men having dinner nearby. We thanked them and enjoyed the free wine. After dinner we went over to Wrigley field. There was a Cubs game going on, and we thought it would be fun to hang out at a bar nearby.

Once inside, a guy soon approached me. I knew he was hitting on me, but I didn't quite know how to handle the situation. Questions overwhelmed my mind: What if he is just being friendly? What if I tell him I am not interested, only to find out that *he* isn't? How long should I continue to talk to him? Clearly I have a lot to learn about the single life, and I am so uncomfortable with it all. I liked the security of being married. Eventually he became straightforward with his intentions, and I was able to politely decline.

As the night went on, my friends and I ended up talking to a group of men standing next to us. I was in a playful mood, and I began to dance and joke around with my friends. One of the guys told me that he liked my sense of humor. He was very nice, and we talked for a long time. We talked a lot about sports, especially golf, and about trying to make new friends in the city. He asked me why I was single, and I told him. I told him about Mark. I told him about the plane crash. He expressed his apology, and then he hugged me. He kept saying, "I am so sorry," over and over. I continued to say, "It's okay," to make him stop. I am used to making people laugh, not making them feel uncomfortable or sad. Later he asked for my phone number, so that we could play golf together and hang out. I gave it to him. It felt as though I had made a new fun friend in the city. Perhaps he could introduce me to all his friends, and I could build a group of new, single friends in Chicago. I need a new life and an escape from my married friends in the suburbs.

August 16, 2007

The guy that I had met at the Cubs bar called today. We talked for a long time, and I quite honestly enjoyed it. I enjoyed the conversation, until I was blindsided with a feeling of infidelity. It came up after we had been talking for a while, and it came suddenly and without warning. We were simply getting to know one another, but it felt wrong about halfway through the conversation. I tried to shake it, to tell myself that I was just making a new friend. He asked me if I wanted to play golf with him. I told him yes. He said great, and mentioned that he would like to take me to dinner after. It stopped me cold. Dinner? That means it is a date, right? Perhaps he is interested in more than a friendship. *Oh Lord, what am I doing?*

August 17, 2007

I spoke with my sister, who has had a lot of experience with dating. She assured me that last night I had been asked on a date, and that he most likely did not just want to be my friend. After we hung up, I gathered all my courage and called him to tell him that although he seemed like a great guy, I just couldn't go out with him. It was too soon. He said he understood. I have so much to learn. How ironic that I am now seeking advice from my younger sister about a part of life I know so little about.

August 21, 2007

I have been keeping busy with finishing my graduate-school work, working on the kitchen remodeling that I decided to do, visiting with friends, and traveling. It is strange to look back on my decision to attend graduate school now. I was finishing up my last class when Mark died. We had been talking about starting a family, and we both laughed at my timing with graduate school, because we had agreed that I would stay at home to raise the kids while they were young. I remember telling him that in addition to wanting to improve my teaching skills, I thought the degree was a good idea in case anything were to ever happen to him and I needed to support our family. He had said that I didn't need to worry, because I would most likely be taken care of financially. I asked him why he didn't fight me when I said I wanted to get a master's degree. He said he wanted to support me in whatever I wanted to do. This thought now sends a dagger through my heart. *Lord, was there a reason that you had me follow through with graduate school? Did you know I would need it?*

I told my principal that I was going to take her up on the offer to take next year off. I believe it is the right decision, but it still feels strange, and I second-guess it. I don't know what to do with my life. I want to push forward by finding a new job and moving out of my house and into the city, yet I know it is too soon. This desire to run away seems to grow only stronger with time.

When Mark died, we were just starting the process of a kitchen and bathroom remodeling. We had met with an architect and had decided to add on another bathroom and bedroom as well. It was all motivated with the mind-set of starting a family soon. So, after Mark died, I had my dad call and cancel my contract for the remodeling. The builders were very kind and gave me my down payment back. However, after some time and consideration, I decided to go through with the remodeling after all, but to scale it back some. There is no longer any need for an extra bedroom. However, the kitchen and bathroom remodeling will be helpful for selling the house, which I plan on doing at some point. In addition, I enjoy planning the remodeling, and it keeps me busy. It keeps my mind occupied.

Lately I don't enjoy spending much time with my friends and their kids, as it serves only to remind me of the life I lost. I hate that it is so difficult for me, and that I have to hide it in an effort to avoid hurt feelings. I want to feel fine about being around them, but I simply don't. I live a life in which others constantly surround me, and yet I feel so terribly alone. There is such a strong sense of loss and longing in the depth of my soul. I want someone to talk to me and ease my pain with his or her words. I don't know who, other than Mark, or I certainly would have called that person by now.

I'm currently praying for
1. Healing—strength to cope with this loss
2. Wisdom and guidance with job and living decisions
3. Certain family members and friends as they deal with the grief in ways that are difficult for me at times
4. My relationship with the Lord to grow

5. Peace and protection
6. Strength, healing, and wisdom for the Wauterleks

August 25, 2007

The weather has been cold and rainy this week, and it has such a profound effect on my mood. My allergies have been bothering me, and it feels like autumn outside. I hate the changing of the seasons for three reasons. For one, Mark loved fall. It was his favorite season. He often joked that we couldn't have a baby in the fall because it would interfere with his hunting and fishing. Two, it frightens me to think of going into the cold, dark winter with this pain. I can't imagine the deepening of depression that I'll feel in my soul when there is a loss of warmth and sunshine. Three, fall signifies the start of a new school year. I feel so lost and insecure with not going back to work, and the reality further sets in. I'm used to spending summer days alone while Mark is at work. What will I do in the fall? Will his death feel more real?

I often wonder what he is doing. I cry out to him, and wait with anticipation for some response. Any response. I had always known what he was doing and where he was. It pains me that I can't imagine what it is like for him. I know that he is in heaven, but I have no idea how to even begin to imagine what it is like there. I long to hear from him. *Just once, Lord, please! Lord, continue to strengthen me and provide me with wisdom.* As I look back over the past three-plus months, I can see answers to prayer in that Christ has held me up (kept me alive, quite honestly) during this time. I trust that God will continue to do so, and that he will lead me in this life. *I need you, Lord. I am broken and devastated.*

August 30, 2007

I met with my sister's friend tonight at a coffee shop in town. My sister Kim had mentioned that this friend of hers from college was in need of a place to live in my area, and that perhaps she would be a good fit for me. *Lord, thank you for providing me with a roommate.* Even though I have mixed emotions about it, I trust it will be a good thing, as I don't necessarily want to live alone.

September 9, 2007

Today I ran in the Chicago half marathon with Rachel, the wife of one of Mark's cousins. She has always been someone that I have enjoyed, and I was excited to run with her. A group of my friends came to cheer me on, and their support made me smile. I found that running helps me to deal with the pain and frustration that I feel. *Lord, thank you for helping me to deal with this stress and pain in a healthy way.*

September 13, 2007

I can't believe that it has been over four months since Mark's death. It continues to feel as though I am living in a nightmare. Living impossibility.

Two nights ago Kim's friend moved in with me. I'm grateful to have someone here with me at night. It seemed to come together so effortlessly that I think it can only be God's provision for me. I'm starting to make some more decisions for my life as well. I've requested substitute teacher packets from other districts, and I told my principal that I would not be taking any of the maternity leaves that were offered to me. The work on my kitchen remodeling started yesterday. It feels good to be productive and to have something to look forward to.

Last week I went to Minnesota and stayed with friends for part of the time, my sisters for another part, and my mom and dad as well. I hit a huge low one day when I was staying with Matt and Heather. I woke up completely depressed and, in all honesty, I wanted to die. I wanted to die, and I was afraid that I was going to feel that way forever. The thought of that terrifies me and suffocates my entire being. What if the intensity of the depression won't pass? Certainly I won't make it if it doesn't. It is maddening to think that this is how I must live now—live knowing that although the darkness of my mind will most likely pass, I will still lose myself in the madness of the dark moments when they come again. I will continue to experience these times when I feel overwhelmed with pain. I've found that the promise of the pain passing offers little relief when I am living in the intensity of the moment. The warmth of light and hope can be so hard to feel and see at times.

Something has to be said about time healing pain. So far, it seems to have healed some of my wounds, but I find that as they heal, new ones are revealed. The shock of Mark's death is slowly wearing off now, and the deep penetrating ache of grief comes on me less often. I still grieve with intensity though. There are so many aspects of losing Mark that I have to grieve through, so many layers: the loss of a husband, physical affection, the possibility of a family, a best friend, a provider, and the list goes on. It seems that as every new aspect of pain is revealed, I must revel in it for some time. I must indulge it, if only for a while. It makes me do so. The sheer madness of missing the person, of missing Mark, his flesh and blood, is the grief that is the most difficult for me to endure. When I think about how much I miss him and that I will never see him again in this life, I become completely immobilized. Mark was my best friend, and I enjoyed being with him more than anyone else on this earth. I miss him so much that every inch of my body hurts. I continue to have to endure these panic attacks, these attacks that take my breath away, and I have to tell myself to breathe. It is always triggered by the horrible thought, "He's dead." I try to wrap my mind around it, to make sense of its finality, until I absolutely cannot take it anymore.

I feel as though I am always running. I'm running in this long, tedious race, and I want to give up, but I know that I must continue. I must push forward. I'm not sure where the road leads, but from my point of view, it appears to be only unceasingly difficult terrain ahead. I want to wave a giant white flag and quit. I want Mark to return. If there were some way for him to return, I would work harder than anyone to make it happen. Isn't this over by now? How long must I endure this pain? *God, are you testing my reliance on you? My endurance? Please let this be just a nightmare, and let me awake soon.* There are no words to describe the emotions I experience, for they all fall short of representing how I truly feel.

I trust that God will get me through each day, and that he will provide me with the strength I need to continue to live this life. However, perhaps the true problem lies in the fact that I don't *want* to live this life. Not anymore. Not without him. I miss Mark and want him back! I can logically talk myself through this. I'm young, I have support from many wonderful family members and friends, I'm financially stable for now, and in a way, I have the world at my fingertips. I am an independent woman, and I can do this. However, I have lost my dreams, my naive existence, my number-one support person, and my best friend. Logically I am aware that I can have moments of happiness again, for I already have. However, the problem is that the sadness far outweighs the happiness, at least for now. I will forever be changed—some argue for the better, because I will be stronger; but I will also be forever weighed down with this grief. It is a deep, dark, and lonely sadness within my soul. No matter how much laughter or love enters my life from this point forward, if given the choice right now, I choose to have Mark back. I will choose him over any strength of character or blessings I may gain from going through this. *Lord, I know you can do anything, for nothing is impossible for you. Please bring Mark back! Raise him from the dead! I know it may seem crazy, but why not ask? You raised Lazarus. You raised a grieving woman's only son. Why not Mark? If not, Lord, I trust that you will guide me forward through this life without him. Please continue to show me what to do and continue to carry me on. And Lord, please let me feel his presence. Let him appear in my dreams. I miss him, Lord, and I ache for him.*

Lord, it seems as though you shut the door to Minnesota. I hated how I felt when I was there. It seemed as though everyone was moving on. Friends were talking about getting pregnant and dating. Why can't I move on? Minnesota contains happy memories for me, but now I need to go somewhere new. I need to go where there are no memories of married life with Mark. I'm leaning toward moving to Chicago. Mark didn't love the city, and I did. Perhaps I will move there in the spring. Lord, continue to make your will known. I am yours.

September 16, 2007

I met another young widow for dinner tonight. My mom had told me about her, since this woman's aunt and my mom's good friend are friends. Given our similar circumstances, we were told about each other and began e-mailing as a result. We agreed to meet. I was nervous and anxious to meet her. As I walked into the restaurant, I noticed a young, attractive blonde waiting by herself. I was hoping it was her. We made eye contact, and she smiled. It was her. It was Kelly. We shared our stories and talked for hours about our experiences. I could have talked with her forever. I had so much to ask, as she had lost her husband a year before I lost Mark. She told me her story of her husband's unexpected death and then the loss of their unborn child. The pain I felt for her formed tears that streamed down my face. I didn't care what we looked like to those around us. I couldn't get enough of hearing about her experience and of sharing mine. Eventually we closed down the restaurant and had to leave. What a relief to find someone who truly understands—to be able to share every emotion and have it understood! We have so much in common it is amazing. *Thank you, God, for this friendship.*

September 17, 2007

I signed up to attend a grief support group at a mega church in the area. As I walked inside the building that night, I fought wave upon wave of nausea. I didn't want to go, and my urge to run away was incredibly strong. However, I knew that I could possibly find some much-needed support and relief there. I was willing to endure the nausea, if it meant that I would find some relief from the overall pain of my loss. I had learned to push myself.

The grief support group was large, and they placed people at tables based upon their loss. I was at the "sudden death of a spouse" table. I knew that I was most likely going to be the young-est, and I thought I was prepared emotionally, but it still stung to see people so much older than me. It just isn't fair. But then again, is it ever fair for anyone to lose a spouse? To lose someone they love?

The main speaker welcomed us and told us about the difficulty that she endured when she lost her mom. I tried to feel compassion for her, but I also thought that her loss just didn't compare to mine. It made me upset.

Eventually we were given time for everyone to share their story of loss. A woman in her late forties shared first. This was her second time going through the grief support group, as she had gone through the spring session. She clearly was comfortable talking about her husband's heart attack six months earlier. After she told us about his death, she proceeded to tell us about how she had recently signed up for an Internet dating site. My eyes widened while looking at her: I couldn't believe it, and I just stared at her in amazement. I looked at the faces of everyone else in the group and noticed the man sitting across from me. My eyes lingered on him, and I thought to myself that I had never before seen depression written all over someone like it was on him. I was worried about him, and I wanted to scream at the woman to stop talking about dating. I wanted to scream at her for how inappropriate her timing was. Didn't she notice the rest of us who were barely able to even walk into the room? I never shared my story that night, and neither did the depressed-looking man. I often wonder how he is, as I never returned to the group.

September 19–23, 2007

Three of my close friends from college and I decided to go to the Florida Keys for a weekend trip. We had talked about it for years, but I guess it took tragedy to make it happen. Mark's death made everyone realize how short life is, I guess.

We had a wonderful time on the trip. We laughed together, ate and drank together, talked together, and cried together. As we drove from the airport to the Keys on that first day, and my friends asked how I was doing, my eyes filled with tears. We all wept. After some time spent crying, the tears dried for a while and then came back again, as they always do. All three of my friends who were on the trip were married and had children. Before Mark had died, one of them had bought baby shower invites for me in anticipation of my getting pregnant soon. I often wonder what she has done with those invites. I don't ever want to see them. My friends must feel so sorry for me, and I hate being pitied.

One morning the four of us decided to go for a walk together. One of my friends had asked another about something her family had done over the summer. She replied with, "It was a good summer." The others jumped in and remarked, "Yeah, she did so many amazing things with her family this summer! It was a great summer for them." My thoughts stayed there in that comment as they continued to talk. What? How could she say, "It was a good summer"? Those words stopped me cold. I wanted to scream. I found it hard to believe that someone who knew Mark could speak such words! I know that Mark was not a part of my friends' everyday lives, but how could anyone who knew him say that they had a good summer? I had just lived through the worst summer of my life. It feels strange to know, and not feel, that life goes on relatively quickly and easily for many. On the one hand, I am glad that people are able to go on. On the other hand, I don't want them to. I'm so afraid of being left behind, of being left alone in this pain forever. People have been careful of what they do and say around me, but at some point they will expect me to move on, and they will do and say what they wish. I know I won't be ready when they expect me to be. I am so selfish! I guess we all are, but I wish I wasn't. This would be so much easier if I didn't care about myself.

On the trip I had asked if any of my friends would go fly-fishing with me. Mark and I had gone on a trip to Islamorada in the Keys during our first year of marriage. It was a Valentine's Day gift to me, and we had an amazing time. I wanted to fish again for him, and for me too. Amy, my closest friend who was there, agreed to go with me, and we hired a guide. When we met our guide the next morning, he smiled and said he had never taken out two women before. He showed Amy how to fish, and he helped me as well. He asked if we were both married. I replied with, "I used to be." He didn't ask any more, and I soon realized that he must assume that I was divorced. It bothered me. I didn't want to tell people that I was a widow, but I certainly didn't want them to think I was divorced either. I decided that I would tell him about Mark after we were done fishing. I didn't want him to pity me throughout our day on the water.

It was healing to spend time on the open water with a fly rod in hand. I smiled thinking of how proud Mark would be; and for a moment, just a moment, I felt as though he was there with me. I felt happiness and pain at the same time, smiles coupled with tears. As our day came to an end and the captain left the boat, I turned to Amy and cried. She held me, and we both let the tears run freely down our faces and onto each other's backs.

Mark, I miss you terribly and I love you. If there were stronger words to adequately express how much, I would use them. Nothing but heartache fills me. If I pray harder and believe more, will God bring you back to me? I've been asking. Trust me, I've been begging. I love you.

October 4, 2007

Alekka, one of my best friends, invited me to go to Bible Study Fellowship. As a new attendee, I had to fill out an informational form about myself. I quickly went through it, until I came to the part on the form where I needed to check the box for my relationship status. It had "married," "single," and "widow" as options. I stopped and stared at the words, my eyes focusing on the word *widow*. I couldn't make myself check the box. After a few minutes, I excused myself and went out around the outside of the building. I hid myself from the others, and I cried.

October 7, 2007

I went to watch the Chicago Marathon this morning with Vicky. The first racers to come by were those in wheelchairs. I was surprised by what I felt as they passed. Looking at these men and women without legs who were racing despite their disabilities was incredibly inspirational. The tears cascaded down my cheeks as I silently cried from the inspiration that overwhelmed me. These men and women were so resilient and strong, and the picture of them is forever etched in my mind. The human spirit can be such a beautiful thing.

October 18–21, 2007

My good friend Alekka planned a "girls' weekend" for several of her friends who had taken a group trip before and had decided to try to make it a tradition. She invited me, and I extended invites to some of my friends. I had been trying to accomplish a girls' weekend trip for years, but without much success. Invites were thrown out, and eventually a group of five was formed with Newport Beach, California, as the destination. My two close friends, Alekka and Amy, along with the other two whom I didn't know as well, were all married. I was the only single one, and yet I still felt married.

We were set up to stay at a beach house, and we rented a convertible. It was a blast. Our second day in, while walking along the beach, one of the women made the comment, "It is so incredibly gorgeous here with the sunshine, palm trees, ocean, and warmth. Why don't we live here? Why do we live in the Midwest where it is so cold?" The others laughed in agreement, and I was silenced as the idea solidified in my mind. For the first time in my life, I was actually completely free to live wherever I would want. The thought lingered, and I decided then and there that I would move. That one comment on the trip had a significant impact on the course of my life. When I returned to Chicago after the trip, I called my sister, who had attended college in California, and told her about my idea to move out West. She said that her best friend from college still lived in Redondo Beach and often had roommates moving in and out. She contacted her for me, and the process for my moving out West slowly began from there.

October 25–November 5, 2007

I headed to Cabo San Lucas, Mexico, to meet up with Vicky and her friends. It is absolutely gorgeous, and I enjoy it there, but it is incredibly difficult too: such beauty in what my eyes see around me, and yet such pain within my soul. The memories are so very bittersweet, as Mark and I had been to Cabo together numerous times.

I enjoyed the women that were with me, as they are all strong and accomplished. One evening at dinner I asked them what advice they would give to me, a woman my age who is now single and in the position to do anything with her life. Almost all of them told me to chase any dreams I may have. They all mentioned that it seems like just yesterday that they were my age. One woman told me, "Time goes so fast, Sarah; my regret is that I didn't do what I had wanted to do, because of fear and because I thought I had all the time in the world." The others agreed with her, and I felt blessed by their advice.

On the last night, the ladies took me to dinner for my birthday. One of Vicky's friends has a great sense of humor, and she brought party hats and kazoos. I loved the freedom of being silly and not caring what others thought. We laughed and enjoyed the evening. At the end of the dinner, Vicky handed me a birthday present in a beautifully wrapped box. I opened it, and inside was a stunningly gorgeous diamond necklace from Tiffany's. She had already treated me to a half day of spa services at an exclusive resort earlier on the trip. With my eyes wide, and overwhelmed by her generosity, I put it on and thanked her. She said that this, being my thirtieth birthday, was an important date and that she and John wanted to do what they could to make it special for me. She said she would gladly give up all the money in the world to have Mark back and that she knew she couldn't buy me happiness. We both had tears in our eyes.

The next day, Vicky and her friends drove me to Palmilla, a fancy resort in Cabo San Lucas, where she had reserved a room for my sisters and me for a few days to further celebrate my birthday. They checked me in and then left for the airport. I went to the workout room to run as I waited for my two sisters to arrive.

I counted down the minutes as I sat where the taxi would drop them off at the entrance of the resort. When my sisters got out of the taxi, we jumped around like a couple of kids screaming with excitement. I felt like a rock star. We all did.

The days that we spent in Los Cabos were both relaxing and indulgent. It was wonderful to be able to spend such quality time with my sisters. The way that they have supported me and loved me has been inspirational. They have held me up through this grief, and I can never thank them enough.

On the night of my birthday, we dressed up and went to dinner at the Charlie Trotters restaurant at the resort. My sisters and I are all foodies, and we thoroughly enjoyed the meal. It was more expensive than we are used to, but money didn't seem to matter that evening. What is money for anyway? We save it for the future, but when we can't visualize a future, it is difficult to want to save. I can't picture a future, and material items don't hold the same value as they once did. After dinner we returned to our room, and, to my surprise, there were balloons and confetti painting it in an explosion of color. My sisters had arranged for this without my knowing, and I was touched by their thoughtfulness. There was a bottle of wine sitting out, and so we poured a glass and sat together on the balcony overlooking the ocean. The evening was incredibly romantic, and although I was surrounded by the love of my beautiful sisters, I couldn't help but surrender to some of the loneliness that I felt in my heart. Everything was so much more than I could have imagined, and yet what I wanted most was gone. I wanted to be with Mark in this place. I should have been celebrating with him. My sisters and I cried together as we realized that nothing could take away the pain. No amount of indulgence can mask the longing for what truly matters. I would trade all the riches of this world to have Mark back.

November 3, 2007

I can't believe that it has been six months. The tears continue to fall with ease. My body has become more comfortable living without Mark's touch and the warmth he provided at night in bed;

but the pain, oh, the pain hasn't ceased. Flashbacks of finding out about Mark's death, the funeral, and the thought of him as dead hit me hard at obscure times. They strike me down, and in those moments I don't believe that I will ever truly accept that he is gone. How can I accept something that I know nothing about? What is death? What is Mark doing? What is heaven like for him?

I'm tired of crying. Although I cry less than before and genuinely have happy moments that last for some time, I cannot come to terms with his death. I find that although I can, on some level, deal with thinking about the specifics of how to live without him, I cannot, however, deal with thinking about the permanence of his death. I cannot fathom how I will never see him again here on earth. I cannot allow myself to think about how much I miss him. The pain of it is unbearable. That is why I can truly live only in the present. The future without him is just too difficult to think about.

I can tell that I am healing, because I feel ready to go back to work and be productive. I can think more clearly and for longer periods of time. It is just so hard to know what to do. I have the resources to be able to do basically whatever I want, and I'm young enough still to feel that the possibilities are endless. The problem is that I really don't care. Nothing interests me. Everything seems ultimately meaningless. I don't know what dream to chase. It's strange to feel like I could do so much, and yet not really care at all if I do anything. Honestly, I want to die and be with Mark. I was at the top of the world with him. There is nowhere else to go but down, right? I must place my focus on God and others, but self always gets in the way.

Enter the World Again
Alone.
Standing at the edge of a cliff.
Alone.
Caught between life in the world I see below and life in the heavens above, where you now reside.
Alone.
Living somewhere between my past and my future.
Alone.

Pounding on the door of heaven. Screaming.
My heart, my love, is there. I beg, please let me in.
Alone.
Everything within me yearns to see him again. To feel him again.
Alone.
I waver on this cliff on high. My toes grip the edge, and I have reluctantly
begun to lower my eyes from above to below.
There is life there. I see it.
Energetic, hustling, vibrant life. There are multitudes of people, and yet I
am so far from them.
Alone.
I know I must enter into the world again. I must try.
I have to release my grip on you, who I can no longer have here on this
earth, and fall into those below who can soften the blow.
I'll be bruised and broken when I land, but perhaps no longer will I be . . .
alone.

November 10, 2007

My wonderful friends planned a big birthday dinner for me in Chicago. We went to a wine bar that serves fantastic food, and I loved it. There was a group of around ten to twelve of us, and after dinner we went out to a few bars and danced. I was honestly able to let go and have a good time. It felt freeing and wonderful to laugh and eat and dance and share life with good friends. At the end of the dinner, they presented me with a camera that they had all gone in on, as well as a book filled with notes to me about what my friendship means to them. I felt fantastic. I felt loved, supported, blessed, and happy. I felt grateful.

November 22, 2007

For Thanksgiving I decided to go to Minnesota to be with my family. The morning of Thanksgiving, my sisters, my brother-in-law Josh, my dad, and I all ran in the Minneapolis turkey trot. It was cold and crowded. The day ended up not being very memorable.

I just wanted, and needed, to get through it. I assumed the holidays would be difficult, and today proved that to be true. It was a day to simply try to endure. I was grateful when I awoke the following morning, as I was able to breathe easier.

December 1, 2007

It has been challenging trying to deal with learning how to balance my family and Mark's family. Everyone is dealing with his death so differently. One family member doesn't want to talk about it, while another desires to talk about it all the time. I have my opinions on who is dealing with it the right way and who is dealing with it the wrong way. I catch myself in this thought and think, "How can I say whether someone is grieving correctly?" Can anyone truly say that there is a right or wrong way? Certainly not. There seems to be no formula for how to deal with this. I don't believe that one can truly get through the grief to the point where they never grieve anymore—at least in the sense that "one day" everything is back to normal, and the person is truly healed. I will always be part of the walking wounded. I have a scar that will not, and cannot, ever heal. My best guess is that I'll just learn how to live with this constant pain in my heart. Like an amputee, I have to learn to function without a significant part of me.

December 17, 2007

Coffee's friend gave the Wauterleks about twenty tickets to the Bears vs. Vikings game in Minneapolis. We invited a large group of Mark's and my friends. As we drove to Minnesota, I could tell that John and Vicky were excited to have everyone all together, as they had always loved our friends. However, when everyone finally got there, Mark's absence was noticeably harsh. It stripped most of the fun away from the event, and the trip ended up being a difficult experience as a result. It is painful to have to endure all the changes in life that are a result of his death. It is painful that feelings don't cease to exist just because we try to deny them.

December 24, 2007

Although I chose not to think too much about the holiday season, I had made up my mind that I didn't want to celebrate in
the usual way. I wanted everything to be different, and I definitely
didn't want to buy any gifts. Christmas was viewed as another difficult day to endure. Mark's family was invited to spend Christmas
in Florida with family who lived there, and they invited my family
as well. I had already told both families that I wanted us to be
together, and we all thought it would be best to spend the holiday
in a new environment with lots of sunshine. The winter can be
so dark, cold, and depressing in the Midwest. We needed to get
away and to try to get through the holiday as best as we could. It
seemed to be a good option.

I was busy training for a marathon, and so I spent a lot of time
running outside. Balancing the two families was stressful for me,
and my training runs provided a bit of escape.

Mark's aunt and uncle were kind enough to offer their home
on Marco Island for the holiday meal. We politely ate together
but without much joy and energy. Mark was rarely mentioned,
and I think we were all worried about one another. I am grateful
to my immediate family for giving up their holiday traditions and
comfort to be with the Wauterleks and me in this time of need.
I am also grateful to the Wauterleks for including my parents,
sisters, and brother-in-law. It was not easy for anyone I imagine.

December 26, 2007

I'm grateful to have made it through the first Christmas without
Mark. I had such low expectations that I actually found it to be
better than expected. I cried, of course I cried, as I still cry all
the time. But I did it in my room alone at night. The sun and
warmth helped to disguise Christmas and make it easier to swal-
low, I guess. It also helped that we didn't give gifts to one another.
I didn't want to go out to purchase gifts and write just my name,
without Mark's, on each package. The thought made me sick. I
also still found little value in anything material. I didn't long for

anything that money could purchase. Everyone else agreed to the idea of no gifts. In fact, the more we talked about it, the more we decided that we didn't like the commercialism of Christmas anyway. It is Christ's birthday, after all, so why are we receiving gifts? Shouldn't we be giving gifts to him instead of receiving ourselves? I used to take such care in wrapping elegant gifts. Now it seems ridiculous. So meaningless.

Being with both families is difficult. The balance is hard for me, and I feel pressure. I worry about how well my family and Mark's family will get along and the role I play in each one. They are very different in how they choose to spend time together, and therefore how I spend time with each family is hard to figure out when in the collective group. I often feel confused about who I am now. I need Mark's help. He was the buffer.

My sister Anna and her boyfriend Pete are becoming much more serious. I'm happy for her but also confused about being single. I'm scared that both she and my brother-in-law Mike will marry soon, and that I will be the only single one left in both families. I rely on God to give me the ability to handle it when the time comes, but I'm also grateful that I don't have to deal with it yet. It's written in the Bible, in 1 Corinthians 10:13, that the Lord will never give us more than we can handle, right? I am aware that I could eventually date someday. My fears that I will never again feel happiness in this area are unfounded. I guess I just doubt that I could ever fall in love again. What worries me most is that maybe I will panic one day and make poor decisions with dating. I've seen others do it, and I don't want to fall victim to my loneliness. *Lord, give me strength and purpose for life on my own. Help me to let go of my need to know everything and let me just fall into the comfort of trusting you. Lord, let me realize that I need only you. You are my Provider, my Comforter, and my strength.*

Last night Anna and I talked a lot about Mark and how his death changed our view of life. I desperately want to rid myself of selfish desires. If these thirty years have gone by so fast, certainly my remaining days will too. I pray that I can rid myself of earthly desires and can learn to focus solely on God. I have so much of what the world has to offer, so why do I struggle to focus on God still? I wish that I didn't desire to love and be loved by a man, to bear children, and experience happiness on earth. These desires have lessened significantly since losing Mark, but they continue to linger.

I can talk about Mark much more easily now. It continues to be difficult, but the tears can be controlled with greater ease. I am living in a fairly constant state of confusion, pain, and numbness. I often wonder about Mark: Where is he? What is he doing? Did he ever truly exist? Did I just imagine my life with him? Reality is so hard to understand! It has been almost eight months now since his death. Eight months! Unbelievable.

I continue to feel weak, although it is less often and perhaps with less intensity. I can think more clearly, and I am able to push the pain aside for longer stretches of time. I have to admit that I continue to get annoyed and angry rather easily. I know that life is unfair, and there are so many whose lives are arguably much worse off than mine, but I still have anger about losing Mark. I had a great marriage with a wonderful man, and I cannot understand why he is gone. I am faced with the decision—and yes, it is a decision—of how to handle the cards that I have been dealt in life. I want to throw my hand on the table and fold. However, I cannot. I know this. Besides, if I truly examine each card in my hand, I can see that there is still good that is possible. There is a new life in reach. It is close enough to see, but I am unable to grasp and firmly hold on to it just yet. When I think about the future, I try to focus on the fact that I'm young, healthy, and have the support of good friends and family. Unfortunately, that is a lot more than what many others on this earth have. I may be broken, but somehow I am more whole than many. The love that I experienced with Mark seems greater to me than what numerous other people will ever experience, and I need to remember that. Is it fair for me to grieve in the face of others who may have never felt such joy? The richness of my life from this point on then ultimately comes down to my choice. Am I going to take chances with the life I have left and try to move forward? Or am I going to continue to relive my past life over and over in my mind and bring up feelings of self-pity? Will I choose to look solely at what I've lost, or couple it with the knowledge that I have experienced a love that many never get to experience? I want to *choose* to push on as best I can. Mark is in heaven now, and I'll see him again soon. Time is slowly healing the wounds, and I need to move forward. I realize that it is impossible for me to wait until I am fully healed in order to make new choices. One is never fully healed from this, and I believe that making the choice to move forward in part does the job of healing. I am broken. A huge piece of me is missing, and it will always hurt. However, Mark was a wonderful man who improved my life immensely while he was here. Maybe he will also improve my life in his death. I choose to focus on that. I have to.

January 1, 2008

It is 6:18 a.m. and I just crawled into bed. A new year. A completely new life.

I spent New Year's Eve with my close new friend Alana and her family. I didn't feel much like going, but I knew it would be a bad idea to stay at home alone all night. I needed to keep my mind as preoccupied as possible, and so I chose to fight my desire to stay home knowing it was best that I go. I chose to move forward in the pursuit of a new life.

There was plenty of food at the party, and Alana's family and friends were very welcoming of me. At one point in the evening, I stopped to look around the room, and I realized that I had known no one there before Mark's death. Being around new people was most likely a good thing, because there were no memories of Mark connected with them. It kept me from being constantly reminded of his absence all night. We played games, talked, and laughed throughout the evening. Although I was tired long before 5:30 a.m. (when I actually left), I didn't want to go home to an empty house. The thought of it was too depressing, and the opportunity to stay out late was provided by these friends of mine. I somehow managed to be entertained enough throughout the evening to avoid the depression that was constantly nagging me, doing its best to push its way into my being. On the car ride home, my defenses finally weakened and came crashing down, and depression filled my soul. I began to talk out loud to Mark, as I sometimes do, perhaps more all the time even. I said "Schmoopy" (our nickname for each other) out loud in an attempt to feel his presence. I wanted to remember what it was like to hear him say it to me. It seemed to work, on a small level. I also find that I say the phrases "I miss you" and "I love you so much, Mark" quite often. I just can't wrap my mind around the reality of his death. I can't believe that he is gone. How will I ever accept it? Will I ever be able to stop loving and missing him as much as I do? I feel so strong at times, and yet so weak at others.

During the day yesterday I ran twelve miles with Alana as we looked around Chicago for where we should live next year. I felt excited about the blessing of meeting her, becoming good friends with her, and the possibility of living with her next year. God seems to have provided this for me. However, I also find myself weak and unmotivated to do much of anything at other times. I'm unsure about what to do with my life, and I just can't imagine ever being able to get over Mark enough to move on with someone else. I feel strange. I know I use that word a lot, *strange*, but it describes so accurately how I feel. I'm alone and yet surrounded by people. I long to be held, touched, caressed, and loved. That desire is eating me up inside. It's such a private pain, and one that only Mark, who is gone, can fulfill. I want to scream from the frustration of it all! My soul is throbbing. I'm tempted at times to try to soothe this pain with the affection of another man. I've let my mind entertain the thought, but I am brought to the realization that it will only hurt me in the end. I would only be using that person to try to meet a need that he could never fully fulfill. I would also most likely feel as though I had cheated on Mark. Even though I am no longer bound by marital obligations to Mark, I can't imagine not feeling like I was cheating on him. It seems so wrong, and I would feel terrible.

Dear Lord, please continue to give me the strength to carry on with living this life without Mark, and the wisdom to know just what to do. Please protect me and guide me in all I do and say. Continue to open my eyes to the people and places that you put before me. May I be used to do your will here on earth. Lord, please use me in a big way. Help me to be accepting of Mark's death and to be open to a life without him. I don't understand your ways, Father, but I trust in you. I trust in you blindly.

What is Mark doing right now, Lord? I long to know, and I feel such a strong need to know, yet I don't know how to get to him. I need to get to him. Lord, I need to get to him. Will he recognize me when I get to heaven? Will we know how much we loved each other here on earth?

January 2, 2008

It's 11:21 at night, and I'm lying in bed next to my dog, Bristol. My roommate doesn't come back until tomorrow night. The house is quiet, cold, and lonely.

I went to dinner earlier with Alana, her two sisters, her mom, her two aunts, and her cousin. After dinner we went to the movie theater to watch *The Great Debaters*. There is a scene in the movie when a character talks about how his father, a policeman, was gunned down. When we reached this point in the movie, my chest tightened and my body stiffened. About five years ago, Alana's father, a policeman, had been shot and killed. I knew from experience that Alana's family had to be thinking about him. I hated how they must have felt in that moment—that moment when the sensation of breath is taken away and an ache springs up from within the depth of our souls; the feeling of disappointment that in our efforts to be entertained and to forget our own lives, we are faced, once again, with the painful reality of what our lives have become; this painful reality that life is defined by death. I looked down the row of seats and saw all the women who had come into the theater with me. My thoughts turned to Alana's mom, her aunt's mom, and myself. There we were, three widows representing three generations. It seemed unreal. It was so hard to look at the wrinkles and the grey hair of the eldest woman. I thought, how could we both be defined by the same word? How could we both be widows? I was so disturbed by this that I couldn't look at her the rest of the night. I was jealous of her age. She had fewer years left to live without her husband. Besides, she had had a family with him. She had children and grandchildren. She wouldn't have to ever be all alone. I drove home from the movie as a constant stream of tears made its way down my face, and inside I was silently screaming.

January 7, 2008

My feelings regarding social issues continue to grow more passionately. I find myself longing with deep intensity that God will use me in a tangible way to make a difference on this earth. I need purpose, and I need passion. I need the rest of my life to count. When selfish desires for a family and for romantic love creep into my thoughts, I feel disappointed. I do my best to push these feelings aside, and I hope that God uses me in such a way that I won't desire or need to marry again. I fear that no one could even come close to comparing to Mark. Even if I met someone and he was different, as they say he would have to be, I feel as though he still couldn't be as perfect for me as Mark was. And although I am lonely at times, God has provided for me in abundance. I have wonderful friends and a supportive family. Also, I believe God has helped me to suppress my desire for a family relatively well. I find that it bothers me far less to think of not bearing children than to think of living without the companionship and love of a husband. If I have children someday, it will be wonderful! If not, I trust that I will be fine without them. In this moment, I do not long for a family. Instead, I desire a radical, new life. I long for a life that differs drastically from the life that I lived with Mark. I want to live life differently. I have to. May God open doors and steer me in the right direction. Life is short, and I will be with Mark sooner than it feels. God has given me glimpses of the wisdom in realizing this. I will do my best not to chase after worldly things or things I cannot control, because tomorrow may never come. I only have today, so may the days that I am given be spent focused on God's will. I pray that I will be given an abundance of wisdom, strength, hope, and courage.

January 11–14, 2008

I ran in my very first marathon! It was after running the half marathon in Chicago in the fall and seeing the inspirational disabled runners in the Chicago Marathon that I decided to sign up for a full marathon. Besides, in an effort to deal with my anger and stress, I had been running like mad ever since Mark died. My sisters told me that I'm a bit like Forrest Gump in that I keep running.

I had researched various marathons and decided to run in the P.F. Chang's Rock 'n' Roll Marathon in Phoenix. I chose this particular race because I wanted to run somewhere warm in the winter months. It provided a great reason to escape the cold of the Midwest. Also, it was a flat course, which is something that seemed of utmost importance for a first marathon. So I rallied a group of friends, including Alana and Kelly, to sign up for the half marathon, and I registered for the full.

I made and wore a T-shirt that had pictures of Mark and me on it. It read, "This run is for Mark. The love of my life." I ran the race fueled by anger and determination. Thoughts moved quickly through my mind as my feet moved with relative ease across the pavement below. I was hoping just to finish. I did, and I came within five minutes of qualifying for Boston as well. The accomplishment was richly satisfying and provided me with the fuel to strive for faster future marathons. It provided a much needed new goal and focus for my life.

January 14—17, 2008

I flew directly from Arizona to Cabo San Lucas to meet up with the Wauterleks, as they were vacationing there at their time-share. I was initially very excited to see them, as I love them and I know that they love me as well. However, the excitement faded as it became difficult to be with them. It usually does, and it disappoints me every time. It is just too obvious who is missing, and I can sense the struggle in each of us.

One morning I ran down to the beach alone and tried to find the exact spot where Mark and I, along with our friends Matt and Heather, had spent a wonderful day together only ninety days before the crash. That day Heather and I had walked along the ocean while we talked about the dreams we had for children. We played games on the beach and drank beer in the sunshine. We had no idea how drastically life was about to change. As these memories played in my mind, I sat down in the sand, turned on my iPod, and stared out at ocean. The song "Never Let Go," by Matt Redman, began to play, and my heart stopped. It was the exact song that Heather's husband Matt played at Mark's funeral. As the waves crashed against the shore, I let myself weep. How could we have been so happy just months before on this exact beach? I prayed then and there for God to raise Mark from the dead. If I truly believe, will he? I wondered how many times I had prayed this.

Flying home from Cabo, I ended up sitting next to John. I worry so much about him. At one point, after using the washroom, I returned to my seat to see tears in his eyes. He tried to hide it from me, but it was too late. I wish I could wash them all away, along with his pain.

January 22, 2008

I am on a flight and on my way to live in California for three months. The plane is on its descent into Los Angeles, and I just finished reading *A Grief Observed*, by C. S. Lewis, for the second time. It has been my most treasured book concerning grief. I relate more to what C. S. Lewis has had to say about losing his spouse than what any other writer I have come across has said. The first time I read his book was this past summer. Now my mind is more coherent, and I find more hope than despair from his words.

It's so strange, and yet oddly enough not, flying into LAX airport by myself. Flying places on a whim and trying out new adventures is the norm for me now. I only just found out the address last night for where I will be staying. Although I have never met the woman I am staying with, she is my sister Anna's best friend from college. Her roommate had to leave in January for a new job, and she was willing to let me come and stay with her for two to three months. We haven't even spoken on the phone, as we conversed solely through e-mail. Last night I received confirmation that she would pick me up at the airport. Strangely, I'm not too worried about how all the details of my stay in California will play out. I'm excited about this new adventure. I've decided that while I am out here, I am going to work on writing a book for young widows. Perhaps my journal will help others to feel as though they are not alone in their grief.

I felt some strong turbulence during the flight, and yet I didn't even feel the smallest twinge of fear. I don't care if I die. Or do I? Am I learning to invest in this life again? Is there a future for me that I care about? Will tomorrow come, and if so, what should I pursue? Will the Lord lead me on a clearly laid out path for the rest of my life? How invested is God in my daily life? How much does he require of me? Does he want me to work in the city? Does he want me to be single? Will he continue to make me feel okay about that? As long as I can't have Mark, I don't want children and I don't want another husband. I hate thinking about that. It's best to close my journal and push the feelings aside for now. I'll try again at forgetting. It's a losing battle and one I am all too familiar with.

January 27, 2008

I went to church today with my new roommate. I saw couples caressing each other's backs as the pastor spoke words that I couldn't hear, words that were silenced by the deafening images of companionship and love around me. The couple seated directly in front of me was holding hands. Like a moth to the flame, I couldn't take my eyes off their interlocked fingers. I watched as his thumb caressed, ever so softly, the top of her hand. I tried to drink it in and remember what it felt like. I looked down at my hand rested upon my knee. Alone. If only I could feel Mark grab hold of my hand now. I'm forgetting his touch. *It's too soon, Lord. Please, don't let me forget so soon. If I close my eyes, Lord, will you let me feel him again next to me? Safe and secure once more? My soul aches from this loneliness that surrounds me.*

Mark always felt a portion of what I was feeling. Things that made me sad upset him too. Things that made him sad angered me as well. We were one that way. Mark was always my protector, my friend, guardian, and lover. Does he feel none of my pain now? Why can't I feel anything that he must be feeling? Does he still try to protect me, even though he is no longer here? *Lord, has someone, an angel perhaps, been sent to do his work while I am without him? Alone. Without him.*

January 31, 2008

I set out today to write about the first days after losing Mark. I found I hadn't written much about the first two weeks after his death initially because I was operating in a constant state of shock at that time. I hardly remembered anything, but I knew that if I purposefully sat down and tried, my memory would come back. And it did. I was aware going into this that it would be difficult to write about those first two weeks—I just hadn't realized how incredibly difficult. I relived those days as I wrote, and the movement of the pen etched words on the paper and sadness in my heart. At one point I had to leave the coffee shop I was writing in because I could no longer hold back the tears. I could no longer control the intense sorrow that was violently turning my heart within my chest. The intensity of what I felt terrified me. The things that came to mind surprised me. I started to remember things that I hadn't realized had ever occurred. They startled me and took my breath away. With each memory, a deep ache in the very pit of my being grew in intensity. I can't explain it. It is like nothing I have ever felt before in any way. So I panicked. What could I do to release this pain? There seemed to be nothing. Absolutely nothing. Nothing that I could do or say, and no one that I could call. And so there I was, left with nothing but pain. No solutions. No relief. Just pain. And so I turned to the Lord in my distress. He was the only one who could help me now. I had to hold on tight to the light of his hope within this dark night of my soul.

February 2, 2008

"Only the good die young." Have you heard that before? This is what some guy said to me tonight when I told him that my husband had died. I despised that guy for what he so casually said. I despised him because he interrupted my friend and me as we were deep in conversation. I despised him for hitting on me. I despised him because he referred to Mark as my ex-husband. Mark is not my ex-husband! He is still my husband. I love him as much as I always have. In fact, I probably love him more now because now I truly realize how much he meant to me and to everyone else as well. I despise the fact that my husband was the best man that I have ever known.

I'm struggling with so much, and people are telling me to slow down. But do I really need to slow down and allow myself to feel the intensity of this pain, the full magnitude of it, in order to be able to get past it? And if so, for how long? *Lord, how long must this last?*

I know I should have good perspective about how so many people in the world have dealt with arguably more (abuse, multiple deaths, financial bankruptcy, and so on), but I still feel as though the pain is more than I can bear at times. The awareness of the hurt of the world doesn't take away my own. This horrifying silence and ache in my heart is too much. Must. Keep. Moving. To. Quiet. The. Pain.

I've been told by others, "You are doing so well. You are happy." A smile, a look, a laugh can all mask such sorrow hidden beneath. I now often stare into the eyes of others, wondering what they have experienced and what they truly feel behind the expressions on their faces. It is true that there is a part of me that can allow for happiness, and I praise God for that. I guess that a large part of me is still just overpowered and overtaken by this depressed, grieving woman, so that I often don't see it—this woman who on some level cannot accept the death of her husband. Perhaps it is the fact that I didn't see Mark's body that makes it so difficult for me to accept the finality of it all. When he died in the crash, his body was burned and scattered into dust and pieces. A million pieces of my heart scattered across a field in Montana. A love turned to dust. If I had been able to see his physical self in a casket, my love as a whole, would it have helped me to accept his death?

February 3, 2008

Today is Super Bowl Sunday. In the morning, I ran a 10K race in Redondo Beach with my roommate and her friends from church. It was raining, and although I really didn't want to run, I also didn't want to be one to drop out. I won't let myself quit, and so I ended up running. Everyone else ran as well, and I ran next to a friend of my roommate. We talked the entire race, and I found her to be very interesting. She is employed by a mission organization that works with Muslims around the world. We talked about the pain we've seen in the world, what living for Christ means to us, running, being single, and Mark. I felt the Lord's presence as we talked, and I was comforted. I felt genuine companionship, understanding, and a sense of renewed strength. The thought crossed my mind that perhaps I would be able to survive without Mark after all. *Lord, thank you for these moments of relief and strength.*

Later in the day I went to a Super Bowl party at my roommate's friend's apartment. There were predominately couples there, and I felt out of place. Although I still feel as though I am part of a couple, I often realize that others see me as a single, as I suppose I am now. I was introduced to everyone as "Michelle's roommate." I'm much more comfortable being introduced as "Mark's wife." I miss that. I miss him. Throughout the party I managed, fairly well, to suppress my feelings about it. I'm very good at that now. Good at suppressing the tears. Good at masking my heartbreak with smiles and laughter.

At halftime I left to meet up with a friend from high school at a different party. There were a lot more people at the second party, and it reminded me of a college fraternity. People were drinking alcohol from plastic cups, there were pictures of strippers on the refrigerator, and conversations were superficial and self-focused. It was another realization of how lost the world is, and how truly rare Mark was. Strangely, the depression that I felt about this was followed by a renewed sense of strength. I became determined that I wasn't going to let the world bring me down. I left the party and decided to go back to the apartment to relax alone. When I got home, I poured myself a glass of wine, changed into a sweat suit, and turned on a movie. I felt comfortable and content in that moment. After relaxing for a bit, I got up from the sofa to go to the bathroom and happened to walk by a photo album of Mark that I had brought to California. The sight of it triggered tears. I felt, once again, the panic of "Lord, it can't be true!" This panic that unwelcomingly visits me time and time again. This same panic that I felt when I first heard the terrible news on May 3. This panic that takes my breath away as it lays its heavy hand on my soul. *Oh Lord, I hate this life without him! Please Lord, please soften the immobilizing sting of grief. May I learn to live with it but not be overtaken by it. Let it not define who I am, but instead let it mold me into a stronger person.*

Nine months ago today, Mark died. As I write these very words, a constant stream of tears flows down my face and lands softly on the paper that slowly soaks it in. It's been a few days since I have had a good cry, even though every day I think about it and every day I struggle. With time it gets easier to talk about, and I find I can say the words. However, I still pause to speak "dead" or "died." They are so difficult to say. Why does "pass away" seem so much easier to speak? Is it because *pass away* means he could pass back as if he was on a journey, and a return home is possible? Those words, *pass away,* don't seem to have the same harsh finality to them.

I often find myself wondering about if I had died first. What would Mark have done? My guess is that mostly likely he would have carried on as before with the same job and same home. I followed him to Illinois for his career, for he made the money that allowed us to afford the things we had. I am the one who is out of place. My family is in Minnesota, and I don't make enough money to afford our house. It upsets me to think that I am more out of place than he would have been.

Where is home now, Lord? Home was in Illinois with my husband, but where is it now? Will I always feel homeless as I live out the rest of my days here? I am but a nomadic soul, a bird without wings.

Lying in bed tonight, the pain encompasses me with such intensity that I can do nothing but beg for relief. It feels like a limb has been torn off, and I wonder whether I should punch something in defiance or curl up in fetal position as an act of surrender. This pain has to subside eventually, but I know it won't let up, at least not for now. I try to fill this hole in my heart with God, but I long, quite honestly, for Mark. I love him so much. If I talk out loud, will he hear me? I say, "Schmoopy, I miss you. Schmoopy, I love you." *Schmoopy* was the ridiculous nickname that as a result of a *Seinfeld* episode we used initially as a joke for one another. However, it soon became endearing and it became routine. And so, over and over again I repeat the words to try to feel his presence. It's so difficult to confront this loneliness, and harder still to realize my loneliness is for the one person I cannot see, touch, or talk to ever again.

Nine Months

There is something living and breathing within me now. And no, it is not a child, the child that I longed so desperately to have with you. It is my grief. I can feel it move; and when it kicks, it pains my soul. Lashing out unpredictably in untimely moments. It writhes, stretches, and jolts, which pains my insides while going unnoticed by those on the outside. Ripping me apart as it moves slowly within, feeding upon my nutrients without permission. It takes all the energy that I have within me. From the moment of conception, it has caused me great sickness: evening sickness that results in tears upon my pillow at night. Life has become emotionally and physically exhausting. I am swollen from the multitude of losses that your death has become, bedridden from the intensity of it all. However, I will endure this pain. I will endure because of the expectation that this pain will birth something good and wonderful someday. It has been promised. But when? How long must it live inside me? It's been nine months. Why won't it leave? It is time, is it not? If only the final pain of releasing it would come, for I can no longer live with this grief inside me.

February 4, 2008

It is a beautiful day, and I am sitting at a Starbucks coffee shop in Palos Verdes, California. The coffee shop overlooks the ocean and it is beautiful, peaceful, and serene. I spoke with my dad on the phone on my way in, and we talked about how I was doing. I said that I was lonely but also feeling the need to go through this on my own. For some reason, I think I need to truly feel this pain in its entirety so that I can hopefully heal and be made strong again. I told my dad that within the loneliness I have learned to be grateful for my family and friends back home. What a tragedy it must be to be truly alone. I am not, even though it feels like it at times because no one can enter into this pain I feel. No one knows exactly how I feel. However, I have people who hold my hand through it all. Those with no hand to hold must feel so lost. Their pain, so deep and throbbing, must not find any comfort or relief.

After I had walked into Starbucks and ordered my coffee, I glanced across the room and noticed two lounge chairs. One was occupied by a woman who appeared to be in her sixties, and the other was empty. I approached the woman and asked her if anyone was sitting in the empty chair. She glanced up at me from the newspaper she was reading and said no. I sat down, pulled a book about grief out of my book bag, and began to read. After a few minutes, she placed the newspaper she was reading on her lap as she began to voice opinions about the upcoming presidential race. It took me a while to realize that she was talking to me. I looked up at her and confirmed that it was in fact me that she was directing her comments to. Annoyed, but brought up to be polite, I took on the role of an active listener. However, I was careful not to say too much, so that she wouldn't be encouraged to continue talking. When she eventually paused, I went back to reading. I tried giving her the hint that I didn't want to talk. I used every physical cue that I could think of. However, she continued to interrupt me with her political viewpoints every ten minutes or so. I debated getting up and moving away from her, but something inside compelled me to stay and listen. I listened to her for about a half hour, at which point apparently she felt as though she had said enough. She looked at me with such gratitude in her eyes and said, "Thank you so much for listening to me. I have no one who listens to me." Ouch! My heart broke for her. Lesson learned. She went on to explain that she left her ex-husband because he was abusive and that she eventually went back to him because she had become too lonely to make it on her own. "Companionship is worth something, isn't it?" she remarked. I didn't answer, and she made sure to tell me that they are just friends now. I was still processing what she said when she thanked me again for listening and left. I wished that I could have done more, and I felt ashamed for feeling annoyed with her in the first place. *My heart aches for her, Lord, and it aches for me too. Recognizing someone else's pain does not take away my own, but perhaps it puts it into better perspective. Please comfort us both, Lord, and show us your love.*

Thank you, Lord, for showing me what matters most. Thank you for the love that I felt, and continue to feel, from Mark. What a rare gift. He wasn't just someone to marry for companionship. We truly loved each other and treated one another well. Thank you also for using this to teach me to be more compassionate. I desire more compassion and less self-centeredness in my life.

February 6, 2008

I find that fantasy has become a very active part of my life. I imagine the circumstances in which Mark might reappear as a modern-day Lazarus. Certainly this world could use a miracle like that again, and so I continue to formulate various scenarios of Mark's reappearance. My eyes ache as they continuously search for Mark around every corner, on every face, and in every circumstance. I imagine the complete joy and relief I will feel when I see his face. *Lord, I miss his face.* His handsome, smiling, warm face. I close my eyes and pray I'll see it again soon. My stomach is in knots from the fear of forgetting what it looks like. He was so handsome. I was so lucky.

This pain within me is hideous and ugly. Certainly it must distort my outside appearance. I feel so unattractive. *Bereaved, widowed,* and *grief-stricken.* These words were once so foreign to me, and now they define my existence. Can others see me for who I am? For what I truly feel? Do my eyes betray me, or do I wear it on my face? Is this cloud of grief around me visible to all?

Without Mark, I am no longer confident as I once was. My deepest pain is exposed to the world, and it makes me feel weak.

It makes me feel insecure. Ironically, I am at the same time stronger. In some ways nothing can hurt me more than the death of Mark. The loss of my best friend, soul mate, and husband. My own death, other than the painful method in which it may occur, doesn't scare me. I would welcome death, so long as it brings me back to Mark and out of this pain I feel.

February 7, 2008

I think about all the women and men I know who are not, and have never been, married—all the lonely people I know who are without a companion and lover. My loneliness is different than theirs. They long for someone to fill the space of their loneliness. They cling to the hope that someone who is just right for them is out there. The cure for their loneliness is a possibility. The cure for my loneliness is impossibility. I must learn to live with this loneliness. It will be an unwelcomed part of my existence.

February 8, 2008

Looking back at the last nine months, I can see that I am in the process of healing. I lay in bed tonight remembering how the night before I had cried myself to sleep in agony. Although sadness constantly lingers around me, I don't feel the piercing, maddening grief of yesterday, and this realization gives me hope. It also gives me hope that I have experienced times of happiness and excitement again. Time does not guarantee that each singular day will be easier to take than the one before it. Grief is strange that way. The process isn't linear, and there is no cure. I spiral up and down with ease. I am painfully aware that the pain can come back at any time and this, perhaps, is what haunts me most of all: this awareness that the smallest of triggers could spiral me back down into the depths of agony. I am crippled with the fear of having to live this way. I try to fill my time with energy, action, and noise. It is my attempt to drown out the screaming silence of my aching soul.

February 9, 2008

It was a warm afternoon as a friend and I drove along the scenic views of Malibu on Highway 1. We saw where the fires from this past fall had burned up all the vegetation of the hills. Trunks and branches of trees were charred, and the dirt was black with ash. As we passed by, the thought crossed my mind that this land is perhaps a perfect metaphor for my life. Mark's death wiped away all the warmth and beauty in my heart. It took all the life from it and left it barren. Nothing can exactly restore my heart to what it once was. However, in time, I trust that my heart will begin to feel warmth again, and that new growth will occur. Perhaps it will be a richer growth, for it will not be taken as lightly. I will always be aware that beauty can be destroyed in an instant, but that the heart is capable of growing beautiful in new ways again and again.

The future needs to allow me to continue to be in love with Mark, to cherish him and the love we had for each other. Must I only think of it in the past tense? Mark may have died, but my love for him was not buried that day in May. It lives in the present tense and seems to only grow stronger with time. Perhaps I love him more today than even yesterday. I am still every bit in love with him now as I was when he was living and breathing here on this earth. I will always love him and hold fast to the love I felt from him. Our love still exists, even though he does not. I believe that his love continues to give me strength and guide my actions. For this I am grateful.

February 11, 2008

I spoke with my mom yesterday, and she asked me if I had been praying before sitting down to write. I realized that although I pray often, I had not always been praying purposefully for my writing before I would begin the task each and every day. So today, with my mother's advice in mind, I woke up and spent my first hour awake reading the Bible and praying. As I began to write later in the day, I realized that I had more creativity and clarity of mind. At the end of the day, I had written more and maintained an emotionally stable state of mind through it all. Praise God for that! The Thursday before, when I had written about the initial days following Mark's death, I fell into deep depression. It was incredibly difficult, and I thought I couldn't write anymore. I had not started that morning in prayer. It's amazing to me how quickly we can forget about our need for God. There is simply not enough strength in me to do this on my own.

February 12, 2008

Immoral men cause me such anger, and I honestly find myself looking at them and wishing that they had died instead of Mark. Why did we have to lose such a great guy when great guys seem to be in such short supply? I'm sitting in a coffee shop trying to write, but find I can't help but listen to two men behind me. They look respectable enough, but then I hear everything that they are saying about "chicks." Yes, that's right, *chicks.* These men look like professional men in their late thirties, and they are referring to women as chicks and discussing them in a way that devalues women. Disgusting. They infuriate me and cause me pain because they make me realize the magnitude of my loss even more. I feel such sadness, and yet I can't stop listening to them. They are so lost. They are talking about wanting to get married and have children, but in the same breath they brag about all their sexual conquests. I listen as one of the men answers a phone call and tells the woman on the other line that he loves her. After he hangs up, he proceeds to tell his friend about another woman he just slept with. *May these men come to know you, Lord, and experience love as it is meant to be, love as Mark and I felt together. Lord, please protect me from falling victim to the wrong kind of man.*

Later in the day, I thought about taking pictures with the expensive camera that Mark and I had purchased together. I wasn't sure where it was, and I honestly thought that I should ask Mark if he had brought it with him to Montana. How can I still think this way, that he is alive and that I can ask him questions as I normally would have?

I found out tonight that my good friend Alana is not going to move to the city of Chicago with me. We had been talking about moving in together for months. She sent me a long e-mail telling me that she took an internship in the suburbs instead of the city, and that she couldn't live with me after all. What a tremendous disappointment! I was so sure that God was providing her as a roommate for me. I was so sure that after California I was going to sell my house, move into a condo in the city with Alana, and teach in the public schools. What does it mean when we are so sure that God has provided something, and then it is taken from us? Perhaps he provided me with the security of having something lined up for next year, but I was never supposed to live with her anyway. Or perhaps God isn't as involved in all these decisions as I had thought. How much involvement in these details does he have?

Thoughts about my future
1. I've been talking to my roommate's friends who teach in some of the rough communities of Los Angeles, as well as to Kirsten's friend who teaches in a Chicago public school. All three of these women struggle with their jobs and plan to quit soon. It confuses me because I'm weaker in many ways and feel a need to protect myself. However, I also recognize that I'm stronger in other ways, because I've been through the worst in losing Mark. I believe that if God wants me to serve him in the city, then he will provide me with the strength that I will need.
2. I was informed that *Better Homes & Gardens* most likely wants to put pictures of my recently remodeled kitchen in their magazine. This excites me and gives me further encouragement in my abilities.
3. I've had some experiences lately with people who don't pay their share for things. I've been stuck with the bill a couple of times. It's made me realize that I don't want to live with anyone who doesn't pay his or her share, or who I feel uses me. I've been grateful to have had a good roommate experience here in Los Angeles.

4. I want to live in a nice part of the city, and because I can afford to do so for now, I will. Nothing extremely expensive. Just somewhere safe and relatively nice. Being a single woman, I don't want to live somewhere where I would feel unsafe.

5. I don't want to live alone. I enjoy companionship. Therefore, I don't know what to do about my living situation for next year. I'm going to give it to the Lord for now and in doing so, feel free of worry (at least for the moment).

Dear Mark,

I read today in a book about grieving that I should try writing you a good-bye letter. It is supposed to help me move on, and I am certainly willing to try anything that might help me to feel better. I'm trying not to exist solely in the past while the rest of the world around me moves forward into the future. I need to accept this and submit myself to God's will for my life. Please know that I've been kicking and screaming as I try to hang on to you and to our past. My grip is slipping. I can feel the future pulling my fingers one by one, so that my grip on you, on us, slowly loosens. I will learn to let go as the memory of what I am holding on to diminishes. I have less to hold on to as time passes by. I hate that, and yet find relief at the same time. I know that I need to let go in order to fully heal. I know this, and yet I cannot. I find that I cannot say good-bye to you, at least not yet. Oh, how I long to heal and be able to live again! I just don't want to let you go! I don't know how, as I cannot fully accept that you are gone from this life. All that I desire is to be with you, and that desire is so deep within I fear it won't leave. Mark, I know that it is healthier for me to let you go and that I ultimately would feel much better. However, I cannot, even though I know you would want me to. I miss you so much, and I find I continue to choose life with you. I am married to the past while living in a present reality that seems surreal. It seems as though I am sleepwalking and don't know how far I will go until I awake. I'm doing my best to trust God, as I know I will be able to let go of you slowly with time. I need to let go of the dreams I had for our future. I need to try to let go of missing you every day. I need to let go of the anger I have about your death. I need to let go of the constant praying for your return day in, day out. I need to let go of dreaming about having your children. I need to let go of longing for your touch. I need to let go of as much sorrow as I can. What I don't need to let go of, however, is loving you. Mark, I'll never let go of loving you. I'll never be able to let go of that, nor do I want to! I'll never let go of the memories I have of you or be able to let go of the parts of me that were nurtured by you. I'll never let go of the love you have given to me.

Mark, you were always so selfless and loving. Thank you for that. You were an amazing husband! I know that you would want me to let go of you enough so that I could embrace life again. I'll do my best to live the rest of my days here with gratitude for you, not in a way that keeps me stuck in the past, but in a way that honors you. I want to live so that you would be proud of me. I don't want you to feel pain about my life now by adding more pain to the hurt you would naturally feel if you knew what your death did to me.

I love you, Mark. I will love you forever! May you continue to be a source of love, not only for myself, but for the others who were touched by your life. May the love I experienced with you carry me on. May the life we lived together become a source of tremendous strength. I am grateful to have been loved by you.

I love you,
Sarah

February 13, 2008

Today is Mark's birthday. Today is the first birthday without him here on this earth. In anticipation of this day, I did my best to make plans to keep myself busy. Grief books that I had read suggested that I make plans either of my own, or plans that would honor his memory. I choose to pursue my own plans. Writing about his death definitely seemed like an all-around bad idea for today. My friend who lost her husband a year before me had told me that her husband's birthday was very difficult emotionally.

She went to his graveside and sobbed. Being in California, I was far from Mark's grave site and truthfully, I was okay with that.

I started the day doing laundry, and then I met a friend for yoga. Two of her male friends came with her. They were new to yoga and provided a good laugh as they struggled through the poses. As they wobbled and sometimes fell over, we would catch eyes and laugh together. After yoga my friend suggested we go and get wheatgrass shots. I jumped on the offer, because I had never tried wheatgrass before. We walked in our workout clothes, with yoga mats slung around our shoulders, to the juice bar across the street. Here I was in sunny California, ordering wheatgrass shots with my new actor friends after yoga class. I was so, well, so . . . LA! I smiled thinking about it. I couldn't believe it, and yet I absolutely could. It made no sense, and yet it did. Mark would have given me a hard time about this one. He would have laughed and made a comment about how strange all the people in Los Angeles are. He would have asked me why I would have ever chosen to go to California, chosen to go where, in his words, all the "crazies" are. However, I loved my new adventure at the juice bar. I loved meeting new people and trying new things. It made me feel alive. I didn't necessarily love wheatgrass, but I loved everything that the experience embodied. A healthy new beginning perhaps.

I drove back to the apartment to meet up with the plumber who was scheduled to fix the hot-water heater. He was there for two and a half hours replacing the heater. During that time, one of my best friends from Minnesota called, and we talked the entire time he was there. She didn't know it was Mark's birthday, or at least she didn't bring it up in any way. I chose not to bring it up either. I was doing my best not to think about it. We had a great conversation about what we were reading in the Bible, and it was incredibly encouraging.

Later, my roommate arrived home from work, and we picked up her friend Katie to head toward downtown Los Angeles. The previous week at church I had noticed in a handout that there was an open night for writers and musicians in an LA café. I definitely wanted to go, and my roommate said that she and a friend wanted to come with me. I also invited another friend who lives in Beverly Hills, and she said she would meet us there. As we drove around to find parking near the event, we passed many homeless people. My roommate locked the doors, and I thought about how grateful I was to have people with me, as it would have been a bad idea to go alone given the area it was in. The café was hidden in a dark alley, and I would have never gone in if I hadn't heard of it. Once inside, however, it was fantastic. The musicians and writers were amazingly talented. As I listened to them, I was flooded with inspiration and appreciation. Given that it was an open-mike event, I never expected every artist to be so talented. Perhaps the talent was so great because Los Angeles is where so many people come to pursue their dreams. I wondered, what dreams shall I pursue? What talents do I have?

I thoroughly enjoyed the evening, and my friends did as well. On the drive home I realized that I had successfully made it through Mark's birthday without feeling much sorrow and pain. Better yet, I actually had a good day. I feel somewhat guilty about that, as if I didn't do enough to honor him. But then again, I know better. He would have wanted me to have a good day. It made my heart smile knowing he would have playfully teased me for what I chose to do on this day. He would have had nothing to do with any of those activities, but he would be happy I pursued them. I realized fully at that moment that it was healthy for me to keep busy and choose activities that I enjoy even though Mark would not. There were no memories of us attached to them, and it was also a way for me to find out more about who I am on my own. Perhaps the best advice that I think I could give anyone else in this situation would be to read the Bible and pray first thing in the morning, and then plan a day full of things you would want to do. I had many friends and family call me today to check in on me. They all assumed that I would struggle through an absolutely terrible day. It surprised me to realize it really wasn't so bad. For me, last Thursday was the most awful day. Last Thursday was when I wrote about the initial days after his death and experienced overwhelming depression. No one knew to call then. No one assumed that last Thursday would be such a terrible day for me, and that I wanted life to end that day. Neither Mark nor I were big on celebrating birthdays or Valentine's Day, and I believe this helps me to get through these days. It is a blessing that I am not overly sentimental. God has given me hope in this way. Reading the Bible and seeing that God provides for those who trust in him has provided a sense of peace in my soul. I think I'm beginning to live now knowing I can't have Mark back, and this is instrumental to my healing. I have realized that I have to choose to control my mind. I have to choose to make my mind focus on what I can do with the present time and the future, instead of wallow in what has been lost. I fully believe that quiet time with God in the morning has helped me immensely in my outlook for the day. *Thank you, Lord. I love you for this.*

February 14, 2008

I spent the majority of the day running and writing. For the evening, my roommate and I had made plans to go out to dinner for Valentine's Day. There is a man at her work who continues to pursue her, and we thought that if she and I had plans, then she could turn him down when he asks her to go out for Valentine's Day. She is far too nice and quiet to bluntly turn him down. The plan also worked in my favor, because I didn't want to be alone feeling sorry for myself on Valentine's night. I invited a friend to join us, and my roommate invited some of her friends as well. We all ended up going over to my roommate's friend's apartment for wine and appetizers. We enjoyed food and conversation before going to downtown Manhattan Beach. There were many single people out, and it was encouraging for me to see that there are many singles in the world. I am not alone. It was a fantastic evening that I couldn't have planned better. I was thankful to have wonderful single women to spend the evening with. *Thank you, Lord, for these new friendships. Thank you, Lord, for your unexpected provision and for providing when we need you most.*

February 15–19, 2008

I traveled to Breckenridge, Colorado, for a ski weekend with a group of twelve friends from college. The idea originally came from my cousin Doug who was also a good friend of Mark's in college. He arranged for us to rent a house and had recruited a group of friends by pointing out that it was a great way to spend quality time together and to continue to show their support for me. Mark and I had gone skiing with a number of these friends over past Presidents' Day weekend holidays, and so the idea was fitting.

Skiing is perhaps my favorite sport. I love the feeling of gliding gracefully down the mountain, inhaling the crisp, clean air while taking in the stunningly beautiful views of the cascading mountaintops. I love to feel speed increase as I move my body rhythmically down the slopes. I love the feeling of exhaustion at the end of a day on the slopes. I love the feeling of taking off restricting boots, removing damp clothes beneath the skiwear, and finding relaxation in the hot tub while rehashing everyone's experiences on the mountainside. I love devouring a well-deserved steak or warm bowl of chili at the end of the day. I love the feeling of crawling into bed at the end of the evening with heavy lids and an aching body that is ready to go again in the morning. However, even with all the love I have for skiing, I had mixed emotions about the trip. I was fearful about the memories it would bring up and the emotions I would encounter by taking a ski trip without Mark. So I found it best to focus on the gratitude I have for my wonderful friends that I enjoy spending time with and with whom I find comfort. I chose, once again, as I continually have to, to control my mind by focusing on the positives in life.

I was ecstatic to see my friends after being in California for three weeks. I missed them intensely and had learned to appreciate them so much more after experiencing life away from everyone I knew. I was lonely and longed to be with the people I knew best and loved most. My stomach was unsettled, and my feet moved nervously as I awaited the reunion. I longed to run to them and fall into a comfortable embrace of pure joy. I needed comfort and relief from the loneliness I had been experiencing. My cousin Doug, who had arranged the trip, and his wife Ruth were the first ones I saw. They had arrived in Denver a few hours before me and had rented a car for us. They waited for me outside of baggage claim, and then we all drove to Breckenridge together. Five of our other friends had made the drive from Minnesota and were already at the house. They waited up for us, and I felt thankful for the gift of solid friendship. I have certainly been blessed abundantly in this area. Pure happiness and contentment surrounded me, and it felt so very good.

I brought my luggage into the house and set it in the entryway. *I* carried it in. Not Mark. Not anyone else. Just me. Then and there my gratitude for friends abruptly faded into sadness upon the thought of having to do everything alone. The thought of going to a bedroom alone, when so many of these friends would be going to bed with their spouses, was crushing. It's not the actual act of going to bed alone that bothered me. I'm much too used to that by now. It bothered me to be reminded of my loss. I was thankful for the exhaustion I felt that night, because I didn't have much time to think before falling asleep. I've been trying to live life that way now. I try to stay as busy as I can, even with meaningless activities, so that my thoughts can't catch up with me.

Every day of the trip was spent skiing, and each night spent relaxing in the hot tub, enjoying dinner together, and playing games. The safe and loving experience of community that I felt among these friends was a welcome respite. We all enjoyed it so much that we tossed around the idea, half seriously, of living in community with one another. It certainly would help to solve a number of problems.

The last night was immensely helpful in my healing process. We had made our way back to the house after a full day of skiing and, as usual, enjoyed a relaxing hot tub together. Conversation went from discussing our experience on the slopes to the previous day when we had received the news that Kirsten and Doug's uncle had died. He had Down syndrome and had made it well into his fifties. He was a lively character who had been the protagonist of many entertaining stories over the years. Some of these stories were shared in the hot tub that evening. We laughed, and I tried my best not to think of when we had all sat around together months ago, telling stories about Mark after he had died. Or did we? Am I just imagining we did? I tried to shut my mind off from those thoughts. I tried to control my feelings.

When we were thoroughly wrinkled from the hot tub, we went back inside the house. I made cookies with a friend, and the enticingly sweet smell of freshly baked goods filled the house and led everyone into the living room together. One of my good friends, Nate (who happens to also be a camp counselor from time to time), suggested that we go around and share our best and worst experiences from the trip. Everyone mentioned spending time with each other as the best. The cold weather, watching one of our friends eat a bowl of deliciously hot chili while the rest of us ate pathetic and cold smashed sandwiches brought from home, finding oneself on a ski run that was too difficult to ski, and finding out about the death of an uncle were all mentioned as the worst experiences. Not one person mentioned the absence of Mark. It was all I could think of, and yet when it came to be my turn to share, I didn't say it. I couldn't. This was interesting to me, because it had upset me that no one had mentioned it. After everyone was done sharing, Nate shared with the group that he believed as friends and fellow believers in Christ, we needed to intentionally pray for some things that were going on in our lives. He was visibly nervous as he talked, and I noticed that he didn't look my way as he said he hoped he wasn't overstepping any boundaries. The group was quiet, and I avoided all eye contact as I braced myself for the words, and ultimately the feelings, that I knew would be coming. He first mentioned Doug and Ruth's upcoming trip to Nepal. He discussed his admiration for what they were doing and how he vowed to pray for them. He then went on to mention the death of Doug and Kirsten's uncle and the need to pray for their family at this time. Then there was a long pause—the long pause that occurs before something uncomfortable is voiced. He slowly began to talk about the need to pray for me. He spoke for a while before his eyes eventually looked my way. He stared intently at me as he told me how much everyone loves me and that they all pray for me daily as I continue to deal with the loss of Mark. My body began to shake, and without warning I doubled over as the tears flooded my eyes and all my strength was taken from me. I felt Kirsten put her hand on my knee, but I was too weak to respond in any way. My body was overcome with the sorrowful pain that had been building and had not been released for some time. The rush of relief I felt as the tears were finally freed was overwhelming. I buried my face in my hands, and all I could hear were the sounds of my friends' tears. After the sobbing had calmed and some time had passed, we began to pray, one at a time, and in no particular order. We spent, I'm sure, at least an hour in prayer. We all cried together, and every time someone would lose it, the collective sound of sobbing from the group would increase in volume. As one friend prayed, he begged Christ to be with me. "Lord, please be with Sarah. Please be with Sarah." Over and over again, this is what he prayed. Although I was too weak to reach out for any physical comfort from those around me, I felt in that moment the physical presence of Christ. I could feel, literally feel, Christ's embrace, his arms around the ribs of my body. My logical and cynical self wants to say I imagined it, but I cannot deny that it happened. Honestly and truly, I felt him next to me, and I will forever be grateful for that moment of proof of his existence and his desire to provide comfort.

I began to pray, and ultimately I lost myself in it. I think it was the first time I prayed out loud in a group setting in which I became completely unaware of how others were hearing me. In fact, I forgot that they were even there. As the words spilled out from the depths of my soul and my deepest feelings became public, my body cleansed itself of the toxic tears within. In my prayer, I expressed the humility that I felt as my friends, who were hurting too, focused their prayers on me. I said that although I often find myself in overly self-indulgent sorrow, there were also times when I couldn't because my friends wouldn't allow for it. I had been given so much in them that I couldn't feel too sorry for myself. I prayed for those who do not have the comfort and support of friends, family, and faith. I don't remember everything I said, but I prayed until I couldn't pray anymore. I prayed until there were no more tears to spill, no more words to say. My good friend turned to me when I had finished and simply said, "I love you, Sarah. We all love you." I replied by saying, "I love you too." In that moment, love was felt in its truest form. It was a moment of intimacy that only experiencing such grief together could provide. I looked at my friends gathered around the fireplace that evening, and I shared with them how their friendship and prayers have truly sustained me. They have given me strength. I shared how, over time, I have learned to focus on my gratitude for Mark instead of on only the bitterness that his loss brings me. I told them about how I often wonder why I was able to experience such a wonderful marriage with a truly amazing man when so many never do. I told them all how much Mark loved them and how I understand that they were each mourning a different part of Mark. The part of Mark that each of them lost should not be overlooked or compared to the Mark I lost. I then got up and brought everyone a tissue. It felt good to serve them, and it proved to be healing, if even in a small way.

I'm eternally grateful for Mark and for these friends of mine. Mark made me a better person, and expressing that made me feel empowered. I felt as though with Mark's love, the grounding of my faith, and the support of family and friends, I can not only survive but also live the rest of my life with a renewed sense of strength and determination. I pray that the rest of my life will be used for good, and that I can be Christ's hands and feet as my friends and family have been to me.

February 20, 2008

I ran fourteen miles today, and it proved to be difficult after skiing all weekend. My body was sore, but running continues to be a great stress reliever. I used to choke up with tears as I ran while thinking about Mark. That happens with less frequency now. I also find that I can say the "d" words (*death, died, dead*) with far less hesitation. It provides me with hope to be able to look back and see progress.

I spoke with my fellow widow friend, Kelly, today. We shared our fears and thoughts about the future. She had recently purchased a townhome that was going to be ready in May. I told her that my roommate plans had fallen through. I am trusting God that he will provide a roommate for me or else give me the strength to live alone.

February 21, 2008

I spent two hours tonight talking with a close male friend on the phone, and the night before that I had spent two hours talking with another close male friend. They were both very supportive as they listened and shared ideas about my future. It has been helpful for me to be able to speak with men I admire. They provide a different perspective than my female friends, and they knew Mark in a different way than I did. I've missed having a man to talk to every night about life and daily decisions.

My conversations over the past nights with such good friends have certainly played a strong role in my recent feelings of empowerment and gratitude. During my conversation with one of them, he told me that he thought I was very talented and that I could ultimately do anything I wanted. It reminded me of how Mark used to talk to me. He was always so supportive and caring. A part of my heart warmed inside, but a dull ache for Mark soon followed. I tried to suppress it as we talked about the possibilities for me to write books, own a coffee/tea/wine bar, open a frozen yogurt franchise, teach, and act, among other things. I noticed that I was feeling some level of excitement about where life could take me. My life that seemed so blurry and undefined was slowly beginning to come into focus. These choices for a new future provided something to focus on and brought clarity.

February 22, 2008

This morning I awoke to a rainy day. I decided to go for a three-mile run, and I found it to be difficult. Depression and exhaustion fought me most of the way. Where were the feelings of strength and excitement from the night before? How could they abandon me so quickly? They are as changing as the weather here lately.

The reality of Mark's death is a thorn in my side, and I ran as if hearing the news of his death for the first time. The pain that made me tired began to spur me on to push myself harder and run faster.

Later in the day, I met with the owners of a frozen yogurt chain. The possibility of becoming a business owner made me excited. I saw the possibility for the franchise to make a lot of money in Chicago, and so I actively pursued it. The idea had been providing me with feelings of excitement, hope, and even strength. However, this morning all I felt was the desire to have Mark back. I just want Mark. No business possibilities or new adventures. Just Mark.

February 26, 2008

It is absolutely gorgeous outside today. A warm, clear, blue-sky kind of beautiful day! I ran along the beach, and a large, genuine smile formed on my face. *Lord, I am so very thankful for this. I'm grateful for this singular moment, this moment of gratitude and happiness, which I know is fleeting but certainly welcome. Thank you, Lord, for the means that you have provided for me to be able to be here in this sunshine. May I hold on to this feeling for when the grey days appear.*

As I ran, I moved my wedding band from my left hand to my right. I did it just to see how it would feel. It stayed there on my right hand for a small, uncomfortable moment until I moved it back. I'm not ready yet.

I came back from running and sat at the kitchen table to go over bills. I pulled out the organizer that I had purchased to help me become more efficient. Anxiously I began to look over everything, afraid that I was missing something. Mark had always handled the finances, and I had such little experience with it. I paid checks for certain bills, but Mark handled all the investing and planning of our finances. He was very savvy with money, and it was his earnings that allowed us to afford so much. As I thought about this, I pulled out my checkbook and began to write out check, after check, after check. Although I had enough money to allow for me to take this year off work, I still felt guilty about it.

It felt irresponsible to be spending so much money when I wasn't making any. Even if I *was* working, I was writing checks for bills that I wouldn't be able to afford to pay on my salary alone. These thoughts slowly began to paralyze me, and as I stared at all the bills, I began to cry. The grip I had on the pen loosened, and it dropped to the table, bouncing until it rolled off the tabletop. I cupped my hands around the edges of my face and tried to regain control of myself. I tried to tell myself that I shouldn't be crying, and that I should be grateful that I could afford as much as I can. I tried to soothe myself with this comforting thought, but it simply did not help. Instead, I only worried and became more and more angry that I had to deal with it at all. As an act of defiance against my self-pity, I slowly began to pick up the bills again. One by one, I went through them and eventually came across a homeowner's insurance bill. I tore into the bill and stared at the statement inside. It was insurance for my wedding ring. I honestly didn't know what to do. One hundred and thirty-four dollars to insure my ring for the next year? Ugh! What? At first I put it aside because I didn't want to deal with it, but then, realizing that the due date was soon, I thought I better make a decision. What am I going to do with the ring? Tears began to fill my eyes, and that familiar, horrible ache returned. I've been wearing Mark's wedding band on my wedding finger. I had his ring sized to fit my hand. Do I wear it there forever? Do I move it to my right hand? I wish I knew what to do. I miss him. I set the insurance bill for the ring down on the table and walked away to get a glass of water. With stubbornness acting as my strength, I returned to the table to write the check. Not long after, I felt an overwhelming need to leave the apartment. I grabbed my laptop and headed for a coffee shop. I spent some time there writing, but it was rather unproductive. I was emotionally and physically spent. Instead of writing, I sipped on my coffee and watched the people around me. A good-looking guy at a table nearby glanced my way every now and then. I, however, made sure to avoid eye contact. Although it felt good to be noticed by a man, I wasn't ready to entertain any interaction.

I was reminded of something a friend had told me the other night. She mentioned that she had been talking with a mutual friend of ours, and that he had said that he knows of only three strong women our age, and that I was one of them. I felt strong last night, but I certainly don't feel strong now. I feel so weak. My body is tired, my mind is unable to think clearly, and I want to give up. No one sees just how weak I am. I'm glad that they can't, and yet I wish they did. I wish Mark would come back and rescue me from all this. I miss him, and I don't want to have to be strong.

When I arrived back at the apartment, my roommate and her friend were talking over a glass of wine. I poured myself a glass and joined them. My roommate's friend was trying to get her to move to Washington, DC, because she was moving there soon. They then tried to convince me to move there as well. I entertained the thought for a while, but not for long. I try to consider all options that are set before me. This is my way of attempting to be open to moving wherever God leads me. I hope and trust that one of these options will sit so comfortably within me that I'll know it must be from God. I continually cry out and ask to hear his audible voice. However, I have yet to experience him in this way.

Soon there was a knock at the door. It was the potential roommate for when I leave. She had come to meet with my roommate and to check out the place. We poured her a glass of wine as we sat to talk on the couch. Soon I found that I was cooking dinner for everyone, as I love to do. We talked over food and wine as I did my best to advert any questions that would bring up Mark. This new roommate possibility seemed young to me, and I didn't feel like discussing my life with her. However, she continued to ask me question after question about what I was writing and why I was in California. She chipped at me until I finally broke and told her about Mark. She was mature in her response and began to ask more questions, now about Mark specifically. As I answered, I found myself becoming comfortable with sharing. Eventually I spoke freely about it without any reservations, and after we spoke about it for a while, she expressed her surprise at how happy I seemed. I told her not to be fooled by my outward appearance. I cry often and feel intense, deeply penetrating sorrow. It is just that I know how to live with it in a way so that it is hidden from the outside world. I'm great at being stoic. I am Swedish, after all! The struggle of living within the balance of deep sorrow and gratitude is daily. The gratitude of the realization of the multitude of blessings in my life does not take away the pain and sorrow of missing Mark. Happy days don't take away the sad ones. I had a wonderful marriage, for which I will forever be grateful. I have heard so many talk about failed relationships and difficult marriages. For reasons such as this, I will always mourn the magnitude of what I have lost. *I'm angry, Lord. I lost something so amazing, something for which the chances of me experiencing again are slim. Yet, I am grateful. Grateful to have had such love, to have had Mark at all. I wish my gratitude would be strong enough to completely wipe away the pain and anger that I so often feel. It doesn't. It doesn't come close. At least not yet, as his face is always on my mind, and I feel such sadness when I visualize it.*

February 28, 2008

Today I went to yoga and then out to lunch with one of my new California friends. I wasn't wearing any jewelry, including the wedding band I always wear. It made me feel naked.

During lunch my friend told me about her single guy friends, and it caused my stomach to tighten. I've been sheltered from the real-world dating scene. Apparently in secular circles it is common to sleep around. Although I am not dating, I don't ever want to deal with that. Mark and I waited to have sex until we were married. This is rare, I realize, but it is what we believed was best. Dating (if I ever date) will be difficult for me.

March 1, 2008

My roommate had a work event today in which they were all going to play paintball. Everyone was allowed to bring a guest, and so she brought me. I was excited for all of it, except for the fact that we were scheduled to play at 8:00 a.m. in a town over an hour away. I had told my roommate that I would go as her guest before I had received any details on the time and place. Although I thought about backing out after hearing the early start time, I decided to go anyway. It is important to me that people, including myself, follow through on their word. It has also become important to me to try new things and truly experience life.

My roommate and I got up a little before 6:00 a.m. The sound of the alarm ringing in my ears was a painful reminder of how little sleep my body received the night before. I had been out late with my roommate and her friends at a comedy club the evening before. It made waking up early difficult. After lingering in bed for some time, I slowly arose tired but excited to play paintball. It sounded like a fun adventure, and something that I could add to my ever-expanding list of new things that I've tried this year. I envisioned running around a field with a fun group of people as we happily shoot paint pellets at one another. What I failed to envision, however, was how badly the paint balls would hurt when they hit me. I also didn't realize that there is an entire subculture of paintball enthusiasts who take the sport very, very seriously. Enormous, tricked-out trucks full of large men in camouflage with wild eyes drove into the parking lot in gang-like fashion. These men owned their own paintball guns and had large belts of ammunition strapped around their strong waistlines. Needless to say, I was terrified! I thought about dropping out, but then remembered that I have not regretted any of the challenges that I have taken on this year. I would not back down! Luckily, I soon learned that we would be playing in our own private group. The large, wild-eyed men would not be joining us, and we would be playing only with my roommate's office coworkers, none of whom terrified me. I proceeded to put on the face mask that I had rented and grabbed a paintball gun as well. We headed to our first battlefield, which was named Bosnia. Nice, huh? We put ourselves into two teams, and the referee took us out onto the field. I have to admit that I hid for most of the first game. The thought of getting hit paralyzed me, and I hid behind a bush. Slowly I began to peek my head out at the action, and after some time, I ran out in the open and was hit. It definitely hurt, and I groaned loudly as a large bruise formed on my backside. However, the pain eventually subsided, and from that point on I took more and more risks. It was a fantastic time, and I realized that the experience of paintball was a metaphor for life. The fear of living without Mark absolutely paralyzed me at first. I was in so much pain and unable to move. Eventually I learned to pick myself up and move, to live again. The more that I have learned to take risks, the more invested I have become in life again. The bruise of losing Mark is a permanent scar on my soul. However, the experience of having loved him will fuel me to live more abundantly in the future—or so I hope.

At one in the afternoon, we were all so exhausted from our paintball experience that we quit playing, took a seat around picnic tables near the fields, and engaged in conversation instead. My roommate had told me that her boss ran the LA Marathon last year, and so I began to ask him about it. I told him that I was interested in running it this year, but I was afraid it would be too difficult for me to drive to and run alone. He assured me that it was rather easy to maneuver and that he had done it by himself. I had read online yesterday that I could still register for the marathon at the expo being held today, and so I asked my roommate if she would come with me to register. She politely said yes, and so after paintball we drove to downtown Los Angeles to the marathon expo. It felt great being so spontaneous. I thought about calling my family and friends, but then thought it would be better to call them after running the marathon. I loved the idea of running it without anyone knowing, and I loved thinking about answering their question of "What did you do today?" with "Oh . . . just ran the LA Marathon!"

We arrived back at the apartment in the early evening. I was exhausted, and all that I wanted to do was sleep. However, I had told a friend that I would go out to dinner and wine tasting with her. I didn't want to back out on my word or miss out on anything in life, and so I went. My roommate came with us as well, and we had a nice time. It would have been a lot more enjoyable if I wasn't thinking so much about the marathon the next day. We stayed out until around ten thirty, and after my friend left, I went to the grocery store to get a banana and a bagel for the morning. It has always been my pre-race meal.

March 2, 2008

Marathon day! My alarm went off at 5:00 a.m., which was painful, to say the least. My roommate was very generous and let me borrow her car and GPS to get to the race. The early morning drive was calm and relaxing. I was even able to find the parking lot with ease. There were plenty of marathon runners around, and I relaxed, knowing that I would get to the start on time. After I parked the car, I headed to the elevators and found myself sharing the elevator ride with a family that was on their way to the marathon as well. I was thrilled to have met Paul, who was running the race, and his girlfriend, mom, and dad who had come to cheer him on. As we struck up a conversation, I told them that I was in Los Angeles for a few months and was running alone. They quickly welcomed me to join them as we headed toward the subway together. The family was very kind, and we talked the entire walk and subway ride to the starting area of the marathon. They asked how I ended up in Los Angeles, but I never told them about being a widow. I just said that I was a teacher who decided to take the year off to pursue writing and traveling. I redirected the conversation by asking Paul about his experience running marathons. He said that he had run four marathons, all of them the LA Marathon, and that he planned to run this one at around three hours and forty-five minutes. I couldn't believe my luck! That is exactly how fast I ran the marathon in Arizona. We decided we would start off running it together, since we had the same pace. As the start time for the race drew near, Paul's family wanted to take pictures. I offered to take them, but to my surprise they said that they wanted me to be in the photos. As strangers took pictures of us with our arms around each other, I found myself smiling from a place deep inside. I was blessed in that moment of unexpected community.

Paul's family and his girlfriend wished us good luck as Paul and I made our way into the massive gathering of runners at the start line. We ran together for about eighteen miles, talking the entire time. This new friendship proved to be a blessing in more than one way. Early on in the race I discovered that this was going to be a difficult race for me, as my body was fighting running this marathon. I was tired and sore from paintball the previous day, and I could feel the bruises on my body telling me to stop running with each step. My conversation with Paul helped to keep my mind off of the pain. He said he was also tired and that our conversation was helping him as well. I thoroughly enjoyed getting to know my new friend Paul. I find such joy in meeting new people. Every time someone shares their life with me, I can't help but imagine what it would be like to be them or to choose to live in a similar way as they do. The world is opening up to me as I learn about the different lives of so many new people. I am energized by the many possibilities for how to live out a life. Paul and I talked for nearly three hours! He asked me if I was single, and so eventually, as usually seems to happen when I talk to people for some time, I shared with him that I was, in fact, a widow. I told him everything. He listened, and when I had finished, he told me that he could tell that I was going to be okay. He said I had such great energy about me. He went on to say that his family was rather conservative, and that in such a short amount of time I had warmed my way into their hearts in a way unlike any other. He could tell that they would welcome me in to stay with them should I ever want to. He also told me that in his experience as a firefighter and in dealing with seeing others die, he could tell how the families were going to handle the news of the death of their loved one over time. He said it was very strange, but he could tell which ones were going to be okay. He said that I was going to be okay. He just knew it. Deep down, he knew it. I told him that I thought it came down to having a choice. Mark is gone, and I can't do anything about it. What I can do, however, is choose how to live the rest of my life. I want to choose to be "okay." We continued to have a great conversation about life, and I felt as though our meeting was perhaps divinely appointed. I asked him about his girlfriend, and he confided in me that he was going to go ring shopping soon. I asked if she had any idea, and he said no, and that no one else really did either. I smiled, thinking of how interesting my day had become. Here I was, running in a marathon I didn't know I was going to run in until yesterday, talking to my new friend whose family had welcomed me in, and having this new friend confide his secret to me. I love it when taking chances proves to be rewarding! May the Lord continue to help me see the possibilities of each new day and to live them fully by embracing all that is before me in gratitude and with hope.

As we approached the last five or so miles of the marathon, I ended up losing Paul near one of the water stations. I was exhausted, and wanted nothing more than to quit. I pushed through, thinking about how I could certainly endure this pain if I could endure living without Mark for this long. I kept my eyes ahead and ran, one foot in front of the other, not thinking about the miles ahead but just the stretch of road immediately in front of me. I crossed the finish line and tears filled my eyes. Paul ended up finishing not long after me, and he told me that his family would love to have me over for dinner if I ever wanted to. I gave him my e-mail address and thanked him for all his support. He walked away with his arm around his girlfriend as I stood there exhausted—and alone. Soon I heard my name being yelled from the bridge above, and when I looked up, I saw my friend Alexis. I had texted her the day before to let her know that I was running. I didn't expect her to be there, let alone with flowers for me. I was so grateful in that moment for friendship. It meant a lot to have her there. We ended up getting brunch nearby, and she bragged to the waiter about my accomplishment. It was a fantastic afternoon full of unexpected surprises.

March 3, 2008

The endorphin high that I experienced from the marathon yesterday has left, and in its place there is now only exhaustion. My aching body woke me up early. I went to the couch and spent some time watching the morning news show. It didn't even occur to me until much later in the day that it was March 3. It has been ten months since Mark died. I had one friend call and leave me a message about it being the third of the month. I remember back when I received many phone calls on the third, and now just one. Life has moved on.

I awoke feeling very hungry from the twenty-six-point-two-mile run the day before, and I decided to treat myself to a large, nice breakfast near the beach at Martha's 22nd Street Grill. I'd been wanting to try this restaurant for some time now and had recently decided that if I really want to do something, I'm going to need to learn to do it on my own. I don't want to have to wait around until someone wants to do it with me. Besides, going out to eat alone has been on my list of things I thought I would never do but now feel that I should push myself to try. Researching and trying new restaurants has always been one of my favorite hobbies, and I want to learn to be comfortable doing it on my own. Besides, it may just prove to be enjoyable anyway. The marathon yesterday certainly proved this to be true. As I headed into the restaurant, I brought a book with me, but decided instead to just sit and look out at the ocean. I listened to the conversations around me and did my best not to think about why I was sitting at a table alone. It felt both intimidating and empowering to eat alone: intimidating to be sitting alone at a restaurant where everyone else has company at their table; intimidating to think I could appear so vulnerable and lonely. Ironically, it also felt great to be independent of relying on anyone but myself to do what I wanted to do. It felt great to accomplish something that I would have thought I wouldn't have ever had the courage to do. That being said, I would always choose company over being alone when dining out, as I'm social. I have decided that I am just not going to let my singleness keep me from doing things in life.

Later in the day, I sat on a bench on Hermosa Beach. It was absolutely gorgeous outside: warm breeze, brilliant blue sky, and sparkling sunshine. I sat alone and watched the waves crash on the beach while people rode bikes, roller-skated, walked, and ran on the sidewalk in front of me. They were almost all with someone else. It was then, in that moment, that I realized I am actually getting used to being alone.

Mark,
I miss you terribly. Marrying you was the best decision that I ever made, and I will never regret it. Even if I knew it would end this way, I would do it all again. I'm trying my best to go on and live a

life that you'll be proud of. It's so difficult! Difficult because the pain of missing you continues to eat away at my soul. I close my eyes and try to remember your face. The way you looked at me, your smell, the sound of your voice, and the touch of your hand on mine. I beg God to let me feel this, to let me feel and experience your presence again. I try to think about what you would say to me in every situation and what advice you would give. I know you would want me to cherish our past while moving on toward an unknown future without you. I would want the same for you if it had been me who died that day. It's just that it is still so hard to see a future without you. I simply can't picture it, and I honestly don't want to either. I'm learning more all the time about what I think God wants for me and from me. Mark, I'm trying so hard to discern his will for my life when I used to turn so often to you for that. It is nearly impossible for me to formulate plans without your input! And so with each new day, I'm trying as many new things as I can. I try them in the hope that through taking chances, I'll learn to live again. That through taking chances, I will somehow land on the right path for my life. That through taking chances, I will find some kind of happiness again. I trust that God will take care of me, and that in time I'll know what to do. As I learn to let go of you, I learn to cling to God more. And this, I know, is a good thing. It is his hand that I am reaching out to hold now. My life may continue to be a day-by-day existence, but I know it will involve a stronger reliance on God. I trust that *he* will take care of me and that in time I'll know each step that I am to take. I've learned the hard way that our plans and our days are not guaranteed. In order to fully live life, I must completely embrace each day as if it were my last, embracing each and every moment as if it were all that had been given to me.

Although I would give back all the wisdom I've gained and all the exciting experiences that I have had to have you back, I will choose to cherish each new gift that I am given as I move forward. I'm a much stronger person now. I've learned that in letting go of the things of this world and of the rigid plans that we make for ourselves, we can learn how to truly live. In not fearing death, each day can be completely embraced and enjoyed in a way that is entirely new. In death, the freedom to live is found.

It diminishes all inhibitions and provides newly found courage. For if one is not afraid to die, then one is not afraid to truly live. Embracing every new adventure, new relationship, and new experience that God provides is to live life fully. I will choose to live life this way.

Mark, I hope that I get to see you again soon and that the life I choose to live out here before then will make you proud. You increased my heart's capacity to love. My love for you will only continue to grow.

I love you Schmoopy,
Sarah

March 4, 2008

Driving back on the 405 South toward Redondo Beach from Los Angeles, I reflected on the day. It was difficult to sort out the maddening amount of thoughts that stormed into my mind as a collective group.

Earlier in the day I had met my new friend at Fox Studios, and she gave me a tour of where she works. We drove around the studios in a golf cart, and as we did, I noticed a group of young, beautiful actresses waiting for their turn to audition for a TV show. As I watched them, I tried to imagine what it would be like to work here or to be any of those young women. What were their lives like? What motivates them and what are their struggles? My eyes caught the glance of one woman, and we stared at each other. I tried to see if I could get a glimpse of her life through her eyes. I wondered if she is happy and if she is following God's will for her life. I turned to my friend at that moment and asked her what she liked about living in Los Angeles. She said the weather and the opportunity to act. Los Angeles is a land full of entertainment-loving sun worshipers that seemingly breeds creativity. She then told me that she struggles with whether to stay in California. She is turning thirty-two in a couple of days, and it is scaring her. She envisioned marriage and a family for herself by this age, and apparently Los Angeles is not the best place to find a husband.

This is not the first time I have heard this, as I have heard it all too often from my single friends out here. They say that the competition is tough, and that the men are not looking to settle down. So many of these friends of mine have mentioned moving elsewhere to seek a spouse. It struck me as ironic, because it is precisely the fact that there are so many single women here that made me want to move to Los Angeles. I'm looking for single friends, not a husband. I then asked my friend if she regretted moving out here in any way, and she said no, because we can't regret chasing our dreams. We discussed how a woman could chase a dream that is tangible to attain, but a husband that she is truly in love with is not something that she can necessarily identify and work toward in the same way. We both agreed that ideally one should chase her dream, and then hopefully a husband will appear along the way. I thought about this, and began to wonder about what my dream is. I have so many interests, but no one singular interest that I can identify as my dream to chase above all else. I need a direction to move in and a career to chase. I'm desperately looking for a big enough reason to move me in a firm direction; quite honestly it feels as though I'm looking for something to move me in *any* direction forward. I continued my drive while pondering these thoughts as the sunshine streamed in through the side window of the car and warmed the entire right side of my body. I turned the radio up and smiled, thinking of how independent I felt in that moment. I felt so much stronger. I was free. Free to live where I want, free to do what I want, and free to be what I want. I am totally and completely free to be anything. Free, but also confused and hurting as well. I am confused and lost within the euphoric sense of possibility and freedom.

I let myself sit in the possibility of moving to California more permanently, and then I turned my thoughts to moving to Chicago. These were the only two options that I have been dwelling on. Although I am open to moving anywhere, these seem to be the only two places that are realistic options and that truly excite me. Perhaps God will lead me on a path in which I will continually see doors close and others that open. I'm trying to accept this new possibility, since I had believed that many doors would open before me and God would lead me through a specific one. Perhaps he has been doing this in an indirect way. It just seems that I have had to take a leap of faith in the choices that I have made thus far. Nothing has seemed overwhelmingly clear before the choice was made. This does not seem to be happening in my life at the moment, and it leaves me confused. The primary compasses that I have used to determine my path thus far have been my own personal feelings, the circumstances laid before me, what I believe Mark would want, and what the Bible says is right.

As the sun continued to force its way into my car and lull me into a contented state of mind, I envisioned the road before me as full of possibilities. As I look back on this year, I am happy with the decisions that I have made for myself. I'm glad that I have chosen to take chances. They have made me feel alive, and I can now see them as the pavement laid before me on this new road for my life. I want to continue to walk away from who I was and walk toward something, someone new. We are meant to evolve in a discovery toward improvement and positive change. And so, I wondered about what would happen if I were to say yes to every opportunity presented to me. It would be an interesting experiment to say the least. I wonder where that road would take me. Would I end up miserable, broke, and without anything tangible to account for my life? Or, would it take me in new and exciting directions that would bear much fruit and leave me satisfied? What would it be like to so completely trust God that I would sell my possessions and wander where he leads? I began to fantasize about this nomadic life, until it was interrupted with a sense of logic. Logic, oh logic, it always appears too early and interrupts the dreaming in my mind. Logic makes me wonder how I would know when it is God who is leading me. Logic makes me wonder how I could afford to live. Logic makes too much sense to toss casually aside. I must take it seriously. I must question.

I arrive home and walk to a coffee shop around nine at night. The people who surround me are enjoying each other over soothing cups of coffee and tea. I order a caramel latte and find a comfortable place to sit. I begin to write, and every now and again I stop to glance around the place. After a couple of hours, I am tired of writing and I find myself staring at the various gatherings of people. I'm lonely, and I long for the comfortable companionship of my husband. I want to curl up next to him and lay my head against his shoulder. I want to feel the warmth of his body next to mine. I want to hear his gentle voice of affirmation and concern for my well-being. I want, I want, I want, and yet I cannot have. I tell myself to snap out of it and quit longing for the unattainable, to quit longing for what was lost forever. It only leads to hurt.

March 6, 2008

This morning when I awoke, I turned on *Good Morning America,* and Diane Von Furstenberg was on the show talking about the strength of women. It was inspirational and convicting. I wondered . . . am I strong? Others say that I am, but I certainly don't feel that way. What they see as strength is what I perceive as my only option to do what I have to do to survive. I have no choice. Is that strength then?

March 7, 2008

Amy, one of my best friends from Minnesota, came to visit today. I took her to yoga, for a walk on the beach, out to dinner, and then to a few other places to get drinks. A number of men flirted with us, and if I'm honest, the attention felt good. It felt good until the end of the night when we went home. The flirting was fun and innocent in the moment, but meaningless overall. I fell asleep thinking about how I used to go home at the end of a girls' night out grateful for the quality of man that I had married. There are just so few of them it seems.

March 8, 2008

Amy and I rented a room at the Roosevelt Hotel in Hollywood for the night. It had a fun, and rather infamous, poolside atmosphere, and we had a great time people watching. Later in the evening, we dressed up and went to a birthday party for some of my new LA friends at a venue nearby. It was like nothing I had ever experienced: a birthday party for three friends in a trendy bar filled with hundreds of single twenty- and thirty-year-olds. Everyone was dressed up, drinking, laughing, and dancing. There was an open bar and a DJ. Amy and I laughed at how different this experience was than what we were used to. Our eyes were wide as we tried to take in all that we saw. I am like a sponge in these experiences, trying to soak up all that is new and unique to me. Amy is the same way, which is partly why we get along so well.

After some time at the party, we decided to leave in order to go check out another trendy bar I had heard about. I love trying new places, and I often spend hours researching the best places to go. I had heard that this particular bar had a great scene, and I knew both Amy and I would have fun experiencing it. When we reached the front of the line at the door to enter the bar, the doorman and doorwoman asked if we were on the list. When I said that we were not on the list, we were told that we couldn't go in. I looked them both in the eyes and said, "Well, can't you just let us in? Can't you put us on the list? I mean, we are two women after all, right?" The man at the door seemed stunned by my response. He paused and then somewhat reluctantly let us in. The experience taught me to be more assertive, as I would have never talked that way a year ago. It also proved to me again just how little I cared for image and pretentious attitudes.

March 9, 2008

Amy and I started off the morning by attending church. Afterward, we headed to Malibu, where we enjoyed a fantastic brunch. It was relaxing and wonderful to sit outside near the ocean. I am most definitely a foodie who always enjoys a well-executed meal with the company of someone I love being with. Happiness is found in these moments. After brunch we headed to Hermosa Beach to try to catch a show featuring Jay Leno at a comedy club that evening. It was completely sold out, and so we headed to the pier to walk around instead. There were a number of restaurants and bars on the pier, and we decided to go into a place that had live music. As we waited in line, I noticed a guy sitting outside who I recognized. It was the same guy that I had met in Chicago over the summer when I went out with my college friends near Wrigley Field. The same guy who had called me and asked me to play golf. He recognized me as well, and the three of us ended up spending the evening together. He moved to Los Angeles only a few weeks ago, and he didn't know many people yet. We exchanged numbers and agreed to hang out again. It was nice to have established a new and promising friendship.

March 11, 2008

Amy left to go back to Minnesota today, and after I dropped her off at the airport, I decided to drive to Santa Monica to meet up with Alexis to ride bikes. We rented a couple of beach cruisers and biked to a movie set that she was a stand-in on. As we approached the movie set, we parked our bikes, and she talked one of the crew into letting us go on set to watch filming. I was allowed to watch them film up close, and I had a good view of both Adam Sandler and Keri Russell. I found myself not nearly as impressed as I thought I would be. Certainly this is one of the effects of losing Mark. Nothing on earth seems so important or exciting anymore. After the filming ended, we walked to a Mexican restaurant at the end of the pier for margaritas with some of the crew. I had asked two of my friends who lived nearby to join us, and they did. One of those friends was the guy from Chicago whom I had run into in Hermosa Beach a few nights ago. The girls thought he was attractive, and they asked me if I was interested in him. I said no. He seems to be a great guy, and he is good-looking, but I am honestly uninterested. My heart is with Mark.

March 14, 2008

My cousin Kirsten had planned a trip to Thailand with a group of her coworkers and invited me along. Of course I said yes, and so I took a flight from Los Angeles to New York to meet up with her so we could fly to Thailand together. She told me that I could use the subway to get to her place or pay more money and take a cab. I realized that in the past I would have taken the cab. Mark made enough money to afford me to do so, and it was always nice to avoid the hassle of figuring out the subway alone at night.

Alone. That is the hardest change in my life to deal with. I feel as though I have always been adventurous and willing to forgo the more luxurious options in life. I just haven't done it alone. I used to be much more afraid and timid when on my own. Now I'm not as afraid anymore. I weighed the options and decided to take the subway for three reasons. One, it was cheaper, and I needed to start acting more responsibly with my money. I want to be someone who acts intelligently in all areas of life. Second, I want, and arguably need, to prove that I can do things by myself. Third, I don't want the choices that I make in life to be driven by fear. I want to avoid always taking the easy road just because I am afraid. I want to push myself to be a strong, independent woman.

When I finally arrived at Kirsten's place, we sat down on the couch and talked for a while. She lives with three other women in an attractive apartment on the Upper West Side. All her room-mates are single, and they often have people over for parties. I tried to imagine living there, and I have to say that I loved the idea of living with a group of fun, single, and independent women. Later that night we met up with a friend of Kirsten's for dinner. It was a nice evening out, and I enjoyed New York City. That said, at the end of the night I had decided that I couldn't really imagine living there after all. It is too big, and definitely not as clean as Chicago. It also doesn't seem as friendly. It was in the fifties that night, and I felt chilled. Hmm . . . should I stay in California? I don't really like Los Angeles, but maybe I would like San Francisco or somewhere where the culture isn't so directly affected by the entertainment industry. Somewhere less fake. It is exciting to have opportunities. Exciting and yet also overwhelming, and a bit scary as well. Too many choices can render me indecisive.

March 15–26, 2008: Thailand

Kirsten and I woke up early to catch our flight to Bangkok. We met up with two of her coworkers who were joining us at the airport. Their other two coworkers who were also going on the trip were on a later flight. All four of them were single, fun, and very well traveled. I kept thinking about how lucky my cousin was to have such great people to work and play with. I felt blessed to be with them.

All our discussions about where they had traveled made me think about taking another year off to do some serious traveling. If they did it without much money and other restrictions, than surely I could. One of the women shared that she had traveled around Mexico and Europe all by herself. She did it alone, and this surprised me somewhat as she didn't appear to be overly strong or confident. If she could do it, certainly I could. I could, and yet I just don't want to travel alone. I like sharing experiences with people. I was already enjoying the trip to Thailand with Kirsten and her four friends. Each one is so different than the others: Two are in their mid-twenties, two in their late twenties, and another in her late thirties. All of them were single, all except for the guy who was with us. However, he was in what I would consider an open relationship. I'm learning so much about people. There are so many different ways of living, and I find that I have a lot to learn. I've been rather sheltered, and I find myself naive at times.

When we arrived in Bangkok, we checked in at the hotel and then immediately went to dinner with some of Kirsten's friends who lived there. Kirsten used to teach there for a few years, and some of her old coworker friends who still lived there wanted to see her. During dinner I asked these friends questions about their experience living in Thailand, and one admitted that she was ready to leave to return to the States. She was in her mid-twenties, and she ultimately wanted to come back in order to date and get married. She said that dating was very difficult in Bangkok. Kirsten had said the same thing.

On the way back to the hotel, Kirsten mentioned that she was going to get a massage. I told her that I was trying to be fiscally responsible, and so I would forgo the massage. She laughed at me as she told me that it would only cost around seven US dollars for an hour massage. I was beyond ecstatic and found myself soon very, very relaxed in a massage.

The next morning we returned to the airport to catch a flight to Krabi. From the airport we took a taxi and then a longboat to Railay Beach. The views along the way were magnificent. Limestone mountains cascading into the brilliant blue waters below took my breath away. It was stunning. As the longboat glided toward the shore and the warm, glittering water splashed against the sides of the hand-painted boat, I breathed in a state of contentment that took over my body inch by inch by inch. Life, as ugly as it can be at times, can also be spectacularly beautiful. The warmth of the sun on my skin seemed to seep through every pore of my body and enter my soul. We arrived at Railay Beach smiling and happy. Hopping over the sides of the boat into the clear water, we hiked up our skirts and carried our luggage overhead the few feet to shore. We dropped our luggage on the sand and discussed what to do, as we hadn't arranged for a place to stay. Four stayed with the luggage as Kirsten and I went to look for rooms. I like traveling this way. It is freeing and exciting.

Kirsten and I shared a room at Railay Bay for the two nights that we were there. The first night I had a dream about Mark. I had hardly had any dreams about him before this one. In fact, I can remember only one. The dream upset me. I was playing with Bristol, our dog, and she ran up to Mark. I knew it had been a long time since she had seen him, but in the dream I didn't realize that he was dead. I remember thinking it had been a while since he had been around and that I knew he couldn't stay. In the dream I didn't touch him, and we didn't embrace at all. I wasn't emotional, and it seemed to just be a fact that we couldn't be together. It was so strange. I awoke tired, and as I thought more and more about the dream in my waking moments, a deep sadness entered my heart.

The next day we rented kayaks, and I shared one with one of the women on the trip. As we paddled around exploring the waters together, we discussed our travels, family, love, and children. She told me that I was one of the most grounded and "put together" people that she has ever met. I'm not sure what I think about that comment. It scares me to think of what the rest of the world is really like if I am perceived that way. If I am more put together than most, who is going to help me put together the pieces from my broken life? Who can rescue me? Her comment made me feel alone.

We left Railay Beach and took a boat to Phi Phi Island. I talked a lot with the male friend on the trip, and he tried talking me into moving to New York City. I was enjoying my new NYC friends, and the thought of moving there became more tempting.

The second day on Phi Phi, we signed up to go scuba diving. Another woman and I had to go to the dive shop earlier than everyone else to receive instruction, since we had never before been scuba diving. Claire was our dive master, and Jenna was the assistant. They were both relatively young, in shape, and attractive. I felt comfortable with them both. Claire took us through the important instructions on how to use the equipment and what the hand signals were. The instruction did not last long, and soon we were all on the yellow dive boat headed out to sea. There was a group of Asian men and women, along with two Israeli men, on the boat with us. Claire began to suit up my friend and me. Once in our suits, I couldn't move, and we all laughed with nervousness and excitement. We were shown, once again, how to hold our respirators over our mouths with our right hands while our left hands held on to the weight belt. My friend, Carolyn, jumped in first, and then I followed. Carolyn, Claire, Jemma, and I met at a buoy, and Claire instructed me how to lower myself down the rope to the bottom. As I descended slowly into the peaceful world below the water's surface, I focused on keeping calm. With eyes wide, I turned to take in all the beauty of this new world. We moved together slowly through the water, and the sights of the colorful fish and coral took my breath away. At one point, I looked around and saw that I had been encircled by a school of slender, shimmering, silver fish. My hands stretched out toward them as I attempted to grasp the experience with the sense of touch. The sound of my breathing created another world of feeling, and tears filled my eyes as I was overcome with emotion. I thought of how Mark and I had talked about going scuba diving together. We had planned on obtaining diving certificates but never got around to it. He would have loved this. My heart ached that I couldn't share this experience with him.

We spent the final days of our trip in Bangkok. Kirsten showed us the school where she had taught. We went to the markets, ate from the street vendors, danced at an underground club, and met various expats. We took a dinner cruise on one of our last nights, and the views, cuisine, and conversations were all wonderful. With flowers in our hair, we walked off of the boat and into the streets of Bangkok. As we walked, an elephant passed us on the street. I smiled. I love traveling like this, with all the random experiences that are unplanned and unexpected.

After walking for some time, we decided to get drinks at the rooftop bar of a luxurious hotel. It was stunning. I tried to enjoy the warm air, the shimmering lights of the city below, and the wonderful company. It was difficult to do, however, as it was such a romantic experience. I can't help but think of Mark and me together at a place like this. My heart aches for him and for lost romance.

After we left the bar, everyone headed back to the hotel except Kirsten and me. Throughout the trip I had noticed the rickshaws in the street and desperately wanted to ride in one, and so we did. We laughed together as we rode quickly through the streets. The rickshaw driver asked us if we wanted to go to see a ping pong show. Kirsten said absolutely not and reprimanded the guy for even asking us, as this show involves prostitutes and is incredibly degrading to women. This then led us to talk about the issue of prostitution in Thailand, and Kirsten asked if I wanted to see one of the red-light districts. I said yes, and so we went to an area where her church had a ministry to prostitutes. We walked down streets filled with vendors selling various items in the middle of the road. The shops on the side of the street, however, were filled with half-naked to naked women with numbers on them. "This," Kirsten said, "is only a small portion of the problem." I was filled with disgust and yet couldn't look away. My heart broke for every young woman that I saw, and I glared at the men as they walked in and out of those establishments. How can humans experience life so differently from one another? Is it by sheer luck that I was born into the environment that I was raised in, when these women have had circumstances that led them to this? Life must have been always awful for them. How does one deal with this? How do I begin to address the guilt I feel? I knew then and there that social justice was something that God wanted me to focus my energy on. My life, and the resources I have been given, should be used to help others who are less fortunate. There is seemingly no reason why I was born into a life full of resources, love, and support. If I had been born into a less fortunate circumstance, I would only hope that others would help me. Life is often shades of grey, but this issue seems fairly black and white to me. I feel grateful for what I have been given, but I also bear the burden of responsibility that comes with it.

It is still so incredibly difficult to come home from trips. The high of living each day on vacation is suffocated with the dark reality of what I am coming home to. I have no excitement about coming home, as I no longer know where or what home is.

April 8, 2008

I flew to Cabo San Lucas, Mexico, from California to meet up with the Wauterleks. They were there for about a week to meet with an architect regarding the house that they are building. They shared the plans with me, and I was impressed with the size and detail of the project. Vicky has fantastic taste and is talented with design. She asked me what I thought of the plans laid before me, and after a pause I responded by saying that it didn't matter what I thought as it was up to them. It was their home. Both she and John have been incredibly kind in including me in some of their decisions. However, it is a bit awkward, as I can't help but wonder where I fit in all of this. One day while reviewing the building plans, Vicky pointed out the bedrooms and bunk rooms for children. As my eyes took in the details, I was overcome with sadness. Mark and I were no longer going to fill these rooms with our children. We will never hear the sounds of our kids laughing and playing, and I can no longer provide the Wauterleks with grandchildren. It is only my brother-in-law Mike who can fill the house with children now. The tears that began to pool in my eyes were hidden as best as I could from Vicky.

I played golf a couple of times on the trip with John and Mike. One day, on one of the first holes, Mike said something to me, and when I looked up at him my heart stopped. In that moment he looked just like Mark, and it completely freaked me out. It happened two other times that day as well. In the evening we went to dinner with their architect at an upscale, romantic restaurant. Fancy dinners, which I once loved, now often make me feel anxious and depressed. They serve to remind me that I am alone and that I may likely never experience romance again. I did my best to push these thoughts aside, and I found myself longing to turn to Mike and put my hand on his—not because I wanted him, but because I was so used to experiencing romance with Mark in a situation like this. I longed to feel touch. I longed to remember what it was like to feel Mark's hand again on my back or leg or hand. I longed so desperately in that moment to be held. I longed to look up and see Mark sitting next to me. I wondered . . . what do others see when they look at us? Do people look at the family and assume I am a sister? Or do they assume that Mike and I are a couple? Sometimes I don't even know what we are. At times it feels as though I was born into this family. Now and then it feels as though Mark never even existed, and that I am the daughter and sister in this family. In a way I almost wish it were true. I wish this family did not know the pain that it does. The collective grief among us is too much.

April 12, 2008

I have begun to dream about Mark more frequently. I enjoy experiencing his presence again, even if only in my dreams. I am thankful for any experience that I can get with him, even if it doesn't exist in reality. What is reality anyway? Sometimes I am just not sure.

I find myself confused, as I have begun to dream about other men as well. I've dreamt of being held and kissed. It feels good, and I'm grateful that I am receiving this kind of touch in my dreams. It is safer and wiser for me than to seek it out in real life.

April 13, 2008

I'm back in Illinois, and last night I went to church with Alana. We hadn't seen each other in a while, and she asked me how I was feeling. I paused as I truly thought about it. I then asked her if she remembered ever reading the choose-your-own-ending adventure books that were popular when I was a teenager. She said that she did, and then I told her that my life felt like that. When I read those books, I would read through a couple of different endings. I liked seeing how a situation could turn out differently based on one singular decision one made. My life now feels as though I am living a different ending—living the ending in which I was never married, the ending that looks so drastically different than the one I would have had if I were still married to Mark. I can rather easily feel very disconnected from reality.

At church I met two women who were visiting from California. I told them that I had just returned from a three-month stay in their home state. They asked what I was doing out there, and when I told them that I was writing, they naturally asked what I was writing about. I simply responded, "About a year ago, I lost my husband in an accident, and I am writing a memoir about my life and grief process for the year following his death." Before I could even finish the sentence, I watched the smiles on their faces turn to shock and then concern. They both interrupted me with their condolences and expressions of sympathy. I responded with a simple "thank you," as I felt almost nothing. I have learned to become completely disengaged in these moments. Perhaps I have told so many people about losing Mark and have been through this interaction so many times that I am numb to it now. I know how these interactions will play out before they even begin. I have learned that I can't always avoid having to tell others about losing Mark. Lately I have been feeling the need to just get it over with. Why prolong the inevitable? If I don't expect to see the person ever again, then fine, there is no need to mention it. However, if I expect to see the person again, it makes more sense to let them know sooner rather than later. It may also prevent any awkward interactions that can come about when people just assume I'm single, having never been married, or are currently married.

At church today the pastor talked about what we feel our purpose for life is. I thought about it, and what immediately came to mind for me was all the lonely and confused people that I have met. I realized that perhaps what we all want, what we all long and chase after, is love and purpose. I felt, in that moment, a renewed desire to reach out to all the lonely people in the world. I felt the desire to love and encourage them. We are given only this one moment that we are currently living. There is no guarantee of a tomorrow for any of us. So, although having a life goal and grandiose plan is a good thing, we ought not to overlook each small moment that we live. It is perhaps all we have, and each moment, added up, creates the life we end up living. I need to be content in each day and view every moment as a possibility to do something great. I believe, very strongly, that this is how I am to live. This is how we all are to live.

April 14, 2008

Last night was the first night that I spent alone in my house. Although I was out late at church with friends, it still felt incredibly lonely coming into an empty house at night. I don't know if I want to live alone. I don't know if I should live in Chicago or California. I don't know where to pursue a job or what exactly to pursue. *Lord, please help me! My head is spinning. You have been with me this far, and I know that I can trust you. You have been good to me and have provided me with all that I need. You have held and comforted me, and you will continue to do so. Lord, I choose to trust you. I don't trust myself or anyone else to heal me and give me purpose. I don't trust myself to always be able to clearly see you moving in my life and to clearly see the decisions that you lead me to make. Father, make each decision clear to me. I will follow you, but I need your help. Guide me.*

I want to live a life of loving others, reaching out to help with great needs, and, overall, pursuing God's will for my life. However, I no longer believe that this requires me to necessarily teach in the toughest schools or live in the poorest of neighborhoods. I have met three young women who teach in inner-city schools. All three of them are quitting next year. Perhaps God is telling me that I don't necessarily have to teach in the inner city, or even teach at all.

I'm currently thinking about living on my own. I don't want to deal with living with a stranger or someone I know on a casual level. However, I also don't like the idea of living completely alone. *Where do I go, Father? What should I do?*

I believe that God has taught me to be proactive in life. I believe he wants us to take chances and to keep moving. Like one of my favorite professors said, "It is easier to steer a moving car than one that is in park." I often think of this. Therefore, I will apply to teach not only in Chicago public schools but also in surrounding districts. I will apply to schools in California as well, and I will keep my eyes open for the possibility of a career change. I never know how God may want to use me, and I need to be open to this. And besides, I like adventure. I no longer long for the "stable life": the life of marriage, kids, a steady career, and a nice home in the suburbs. That life is no more secure than any other. It is a false illusion. Death can come to anyone at any time. It affects rich and poor alike. I'm not advocating poor and reckless decision making, such as spending all of one's savings, but I am advocating the awareness that everything, including our own life, is on loan. We will leave this world with nothing. We will walk out of this world alone.

April 20, 2008

I woke to the news that my sister Anna got engaged last night. I'm excited for her, but also sad for me. It comes with mixed emotions, as I don't have a firm grasp on my exact feelings. It seems to take me a while to let everything sink in. I am a slow processor.

I went to church this morning with John and Vicky as well as Mark's aunt and uncle who were in town. Vicky told me that the uncle had mentioned to her that I should remarry soon because I am young and attractive. Exactly who does he think that I should marry? I find this to be ridiculous and ignorant. I know he means well, but it upset me anyway. I experience the perception that others want to "fix" my problem by setting me up with any single men that they know.

That evening I went to my church in the city. It was a small group that attended, and we went around in a circle sharing the gifts and talents that we thought God wanted us to be using right now. My immediate thought was the perspective of life that I have gained from losing Mark. I decided that I was going to, for the first time in a group setting, share about losing my husband. As I thought about what I would say, I began to shake with nervousness. My voice was unstable, and I couldn't make much eye contact with others, even though I was able to get through the story. When I had finished, I looked up, and many thanked me for sharing. A number of women came up to me after and told me how strong I appeared. "I would never have known," one said to me with tears in her eyes. "You have this joy about you, and I would never have even guessed." This is not the first time that I have heard this. A guy that one of my friends is dating once told her that "if you were to say that someone in this room lost her husband, I would pick Sarah out last." It makes me think of how a cousin of mine, who hasn't talked to me in months, apparently told her mother that I am doing fine. She had come to this conclusion solely based on what she had seen on my Facebook page. My mom told me this, and I laughed, thinking, "Who is going to put pictures of themselves crying and depressed on Facebook?" I realize that I can hide my emotions well, further proving that people never know what someone has been through by just looking at them. Appearances are so deceiving.

As I continued to talk with other women at church that night, I was able to make a few connections for possible future living situations. Two friends of mine from church told me that their third roommate would be leaving in June. Another friend informed me of a girl that she knows who is looking for a roommate. *Lord, thank you for providing possibilities.* I continue to think about living alone versus with a roommate. I also continue to consider Chicago versus California. I'm praying about it and trying my best to see where I am led.

April 22, 2008

I woke up incredibly tired today. Many times I find my body and mind to be completely exhausted. I simply desired to lie down and do nothing with the day. However, I have so much to do! I have to sell the house, determine where to move, find a job, find a place to live, and figure out what I am going to do with everything that I own. It is so overwhelming. Running, which was once my outlet for stress, has become difficult lately. Where is the anger that once fueled me? It is there on some level, but now I find that I am just tired. *I'm so tired, Lord.*

I dreamt about Mark again last night. I dreamt that I was on vacation with some women and that the men were going to meet us later, but they were late. I was anxious for Mark to get there, and in the dream we were going through a difficult time. I wasn't exactly sure what was going on. We weren't divorced, but we weren't together either. We were separated, I think. Perhaps this dream is my subconscious mind trying to come to terms with what I am. I am widowed: no longer married but not completely single either.

April 25, 2008

A friend came to visit me for the weekend. While with me, she talked incessantly about men and trying to find a husband. It didn't take long before I became annoyed. Certainly there is more to life than chasing after romance and love. There has to be! *Please, Lord, there has to be more.* Listening to her made me nervous about dating. In the evening we went out to dinner and to explore the city. I was able to have a good time and to enjoy the evening with my friend. However, filling my time with self-indulgent fun isn't as fulfilling as meaningful conversations and actions. How will I be able to find balance of these things in life?

April 27, 2008

Today I cleaned out the basement and garage with my good friend Alekka who lives in the area. We hauled big items out to the front lawn for the trash pickup the next day. As I struggled to drag the heavy items across the lawn, my thoughts turned to how this would have been Mark's job. It made me feel sad, yet at the same time it empowered me to know that I can do it on my own. I am beginning to feel anxious, and I'm becoming manic about wanting to get rid of everything in the hopes that maybe it will help me to heal faster. I'll do whatever it takes.

I drove to church by myself, and as I did, my mind was bombarded repeatedly with thoughts of Mark. Tears filled my eyes and made it difficult to drive. I still can't believe that he is gone. I struggle to move forward. I hate that I have to sell the house, find a job, live alone, and find a new life for myself.

After church I found myself in a deep discussion with one of the men who preaches from time to time. I appreciated being able to talk with another man about serious issues in life such as faith and death. It felt good to engage in conversations at this level. I wish that I could talk on this level with Mike and John. I wish that I could talk to them about Mark, but they don't appear to want to, as they hardly mention his name.

April 28, 2008

I drove to the school where I had worked to meet up with my former coworkers for lunch. On my way there, anxiety and anger grew within me as I thought about my life before May 3, 2007. I wanted to go back to my life at that point, and I was angry that I couldn't. The idea of turning the car around tempted me, but I continued to drive forward. I continue to have to push forward. It is a constant and difficult daily decision to continually move toward a new life. Once I arrived at the school building, I felt better. I had made it, and I was proud of myself for not turning around and giving up.

Later in the day, John and Mike came over to the house to go through Mark's things. I could see how much they were struggling. Eventually John could fight it no longer, and the tears streamed down his face. He apologized for crying, and I pleaded with him not to apologize. We embraced, and I was glad that he was opening up. He soon left, but Mike stayed for a while, and we had a long conversation while sitting on the hallway floor. It was honest and heartfelt. I was so grateful for their willingness to open up to me today. *Thank you, Lord.*

May 1, 2008

My sister Kim flew in to spend the weekend with me. I picked her up at 8:30 in the evening, and we headed to the city for dinner at Sushi Wabi, one of my favorite restaurants in Chicago. The place was packed. I love the energy that is experienced within a crowd of people. It excites me. After dinner we walked around Old Town, an area of the city that I enjoy and where I would like to potentially live. We stopped to have a glass of wine at a bar with outside seating, and we enjoyed the fresh air as we conversed about life. When the conversation turned to what I wanted to do in my own life, we went back and forth discussing owning a wine/coffee shop versus teaching, as well as California versus Chicago. I expressed to my sister that I continue to feel very unsure, and she responded by asking if I knew what to do based on what I felt in my gut. She said that she feels as though most of us know the answer deep within. I sat there for a while processing what she said and realized that I was leaning more toward Chicago. It makes sense for now. I will be closer to my family and to Mark's family. In addition, I feel as though I would be more likely to meet people with a similar mind-set here rather than in California. The conversation then turned to my sister's life, and she told me how they had just purchased a Lexus. She was very excited about it, and I was surprised to experience annoyance listening to her talk about a car. I knew it was normal for her to be excited about what she was sharing with me, and so I hid my feelings about the subject. I bounce back and forth between caring about material items and being annoyed by them. I struggle to reenter the world.

May 2, 2008

My parents arrived at my house around noon, and we went straight to a restaurant in town for lunch. Alana, perhaps my closest friend that I had made since Mark died, came with us. It was meaningful for my family to meet her, as she has become so much a part of my life now. We spent the afternoon walking around Glen Ellyn and relaxing together. Later that evening at dinner, I asked my family what makes them excited about life. They shared and then asked me the same question. As I sorted through my feelings in an attempt to verbalize them, I realized how much fulfillment I have found in new experiences. It rejuvenates me to take chances and seek out adventures in life— perhaps because it somehow proves that I can make it on my own, that I can survive in this life without Mark. Or perhaps it is because I need to focus my mind on things that have nothing to do with Mark. It provides a small sense of relief. I think that this is why I have been experiencing such a strong aversion to living a predictable and mundane existence. Predictable was the life that I used to live with Mark, or so I once thought. Or perhaps my desire to experience new things comes from wanting to feel the pride that I know Mark would feel if he could see me. I feel as though I have a good understanding of who I am, and yet I struggle so much at times to pinpoint the smallest things about my feelings and desires.

I felt it important to express to my parents just how grateful that I am for having grown up in an environment where I felt loved and supported. I don't know why I have been so lucky to have that and also to have the love of such a wonderful man. People are constantly searching for the love that I once had. Although Mark is now gone, his love isn't. It may sound cliché, but it is truth to me. I can often hear what he would say to me. I can hear his words as I continue to live this life, and I am grateful for that. So grateful, in fact, that I would marry him all over again. I would marry him knowing that it would end this way and that I would live with the pain of missing him. I have been struck with how life is all about choice and how little control we actually have. Our gender, our family, where we are born, the aptitudes and talents that we have, are not of our choice. We were born with them. However, what we do with them and the choices that we make in each moment are up to us. I have to choose every day how to view my life's circumstances and how to respond to them. I choose how I spend my time. I realize that I can either focus on my loss and the intensity of it, or I can choose to focus on how I was able to experience true love and how it has made me a stronger person forever. As I shared this insight with my parents, the tears flowed collectively. We cried for a long time together, and although I was aware that our server noticed this and it made me self-conscious, I also knew that it was necessary. It helped to heal me and to heal the relationships in my family. I felt significantly closer to my mom and dad in those moments. After dinner we went back to my house, and my close friends Matt and Heather were there. They had driven from Minnesota to Glen Ellyn for the anniversary of Mark's death. We stayed up late talking and sharing in the comfort of one another's company. I felt blessed to have such close friends and family.

May 3, 2008

My sister Kim and my dog, Bristol, slept with me in my bed. My dad and Matt woke early to go golfing with John and Mike. My mom, Kim, Heather, and I walked into town to get some coffee. We then spent the day organizing the basement and garage. Vicky came over to plant flowers in the urns out front. It was nice to be productive and to have our minds focused on things that needed to get done. I so desperately want to sell the house.

We took a break from the work to eat lunch together at a restaurant in town. When we returned, the guys were back from golfing, and they joined in to help with what needed to get done around the house. I asked Matt to help me make a list of Mark's things that I could give to different friends of his. He took some of Mark's hats from the closet, and as he moved his hands slowly and carefully across them, he reminisced about the years in which Mark had worn each one. His memory was fantastic and full of detail. I appreciated it and hung on to every detail he shared, every word he said. Heather soon joined us at the dining table as we continued to re-create the memories. I went to the kitchen and came back to pour us each a glass of wine. We sipped the wine as we drank in the sweetness of each story of Mark shared. There were tears, smiles, and laughter.

A bit later in the evening Joe and Paige, our neighbors, stopped by with an ice-cream cake from Dairy Queen. Mark and I both loved Dairy Queen cakes, and we had often bought them for special occasions. It was so thoughtful of them to bring one over today. They have been such close friends of ours, and it saddens me to experience some distance from Joe since Mark's death. Paige told me that he doesn't talk about Mark.

Time flew by as we continued to relive the memories, and sooner than I wanted, we had to leave for dinner in the city. I had made reservations for my family, Mark's family, Matt and Heather, and myself at a Moroccan restaurant in Chicago. They had reserved a private room for us, and we sat around a large table on the floor. I wanted to try something different, in an attempt to make a new memory. I certainly didn't want to eat at a rigid and formal restaurant. Not today. It needed to be conducive to creating a positive and lighthearted mood.

After the dinner my parents, Matt, Heather, and I went to a jazz club. It turned out to be surprisingly enjoyable, and we stayed out until midnight. I had been carefully watching the clock and was relieved when it turned midnight. I made it! I survived through the full year, through every anniversary. Will things be easier now? When we returned to my home, everyone went to sleep except for Heather and me. We stayed up until after three in the morning talking about many things and just sharing life in general. She mentioned that some people have been asking if I've started dating yet. I knew it would be coming soon, that people would start to ask me about dating. I wish it were that easy and that one day I could just decide to date and everything would be okay. I wonder what the next year will be like. Will I date? Will I move? Will I start an entirely new career? Will I be happy?

Mark,

You would be so very proud of your parents, my family, and our friends. Even though there have been ups and downs, they have taken such great care of me, and I have felt a tremendous amount of love from them. I know that you would not be surprised at this, and that you would smile. They miss you so much, and my heart breaks for them. It breaks for all of us. We struggle to find ways to comfort one another, and yet we all fall short.

Life can be so painful without you. It amazes me how the simple act of falling in love with you has forever altered my life for the worse, but also for the better. You were a gift to us all, and this is why it must hurt so much to be without you. We love you and miss you.

Concluding Remarks at the End of a Year

I'm not at all healed. Not even close. However, I am now used to sleeping alone, eating alone, making decisions on my own, and living without the physical affection of a man. I have taken the first steps in this life without Mark, and I am doing the best I can. I become stronger with time, and yet I find that I continue to easily weaken upon the mere thought of him. Perhaps it's not that I'm actually stronger, but just that in time the pain is suppressed deeper within me as the days go by and I get more used to living this way. I can withstand more pain, and I know how to endure difficulty. My body now endures a continual vague general discomfort instead of constant piercing, stabbing pain. The need to touch Mark, talk to him, and experience his presence is overall lessened. I have taken off my wedding ring but continue to wear his band, switching it from my left hand to my right and back again. I also continue to sleep on the right side of the bed, with enough room for him on my left, where he once was. It isn't a conscious decision, just a habit, even though I continue to feel as though this nightmare will end and that I will awake soon to find him here again.

I notice couples everywhere. Their caresses and sweet embraces are at times painful to me. I try to ignore them and the envious feelings that arise. Can I survive without affection and suppress the longing that I feel? Can I endure it for the rest of my life? Can I endure this imposed celibacy? I believe I can, with God's help and with knowing I've made it thus far.

I am a walking paradox. I want to make the most of each day, and yet I also want time to pass quickly so that I am closer to reuniting with him. My entire being continues to be a walking battlefield. Joy, pain, envy, sorrow, gratitude, and peace fight for my mind and soul. The complexity of my varying emotions, thoughts, and actions creates a dizzying life, and my arms reach like branches for stability. People who meet me say that I appear strong and happy. My life is like a quilt. The front is pieced together in an aesthetically pleasing way, and yet the back, the side that most don't see, is messy and frayed. I live feeling both joy and pain simultaneously.

Within the walls of my heart there is a void that will forever throb with the pain of aching for Mark. I believe I will always be inconveniently reminded of his loss in unexpected ways. It seems as though just when I feel strong, the remembrance of him weakens me in ways I cannot control and reminds me of the permanence of death.

Perhaps someday I will hardly believe that I was ever even married and that Mark existed at all. At times I already wonder if I dreamt it all. Am I accurately remembering him and our marriage? Was it as wonderful as I remember, or am I idealizing it because death can do that? I believe that he was wonderful, and so was our life together. I will be forever grateful that Mark's soul and his very being have been forever grafted on mine. He has made me a better person. He has improved all of us who knew him. Mark is gone, and I can't change that. What I can do, however, is choose how to live the rest of my life without him.

Oh Lord, how I loved him and love him still. Thank you for the blessing of our marriage. Thank you for the experience of loving him and being loved by him. May I live in the freedom of this gratitude instead of in the restricting chains of grief. May my sorrow be overcome by your incomprehensible peace. Thank you that your grace comes in the hour of greatest need and not just in the anticipation of it. Thank you for the times when you grant me newfound excitement in life. Thank you for new friends and new adventures. Thank you that when I cry out to you for answers, you give yourself to me, and that can be, and is, enough. Thank you for allowing me to be angry that Mark is gone, and thank you for allowing me to question it. Thank you for the strength that you give me to live each day. Although life isn't easy or comfortable, I am grateful for the joy you give. You are the great Comforter. Continue to comfort us all, as we will continue to miss Mark forever.

I wrote this for a friend who lost her husband and son in a fire. She was left a widow and single mother with two little girls.

If I could take the pain away, I would bear it all for you.
This is nothing that you and your precious girls should ever go through.
I'll pray day and night for God's peace to lie like a blanket on your soul, to wrap you up and keep you warm, to give you comfort in this storm.
Rest in him, sweet girl, rest.

Every morning when you find yourself hoping to awake from this nightmare, you pray that it is not true, and there is little comfort in what others can do. Feel God's arms wrapped around you and rest.
Rest in him, sweet girl, rest.

You ache to be with them, and everything in you longs for heaven and for home. You no longer care for what this world has to offer—without the other half of your soul and your heart. When all feels meaningless and you are overcome with despair because you are apart, rest in him, sweet girl, rest.

When the pain builds until it is too much to endure and you erupt in tears and screams, and when you are angry with God because you have lost all your hopes and dreams, let it all out and cry on the shoulders of those who care: your friends and family who are here to help with the pain you have to bear. Rest in him, sweet girl, rest.

When it feels as though all is lost and you don't know what to do, and nothing, nothing is of any interest to you,
feel his strength holding you close and his tender arms caressing your precious head as you lay it all down day by day. Stare into his face and let this world fade away.
Rest in him, sweet girl, rest.

I pray for you to physically feel God's arms around you as I did in my deepest moment of despair.

Since this book was written almost four years ago, I have done the following:

1. Sold my home in Glen Ellyn, moved to downtown Chicago for a year and then to California
2. Taken a year of improv classes at Second City
3. Worked at a coffee shop in downtown Chicago to see if I would want to own one someday
4. Worked for a university in Chicago as a student-teacher supervisor
5. Volunteered as a tutor for an inner-city after-school program
6. Continued to travel the world
7. Dated and experienced love again
8. Run five more marathons, including the Boston Marathon, as well as numerous other races
9. Taken photography classes at colleges in Chicago and California
10. Was featured as a semifinalist and a founder's favorite for RAW artists for my photography
11. Started taking photographs for nonprofits and developed Sarah Wauterlek Photography (www.sarahwauterlekphotography.com)
12. Cofounded a business, Travelers Gift Vacations, which combines luxury travel with purpose (www.travelersgiftvacations.com)
13. Participated in the training to become a workout instructor
14. Continued to meet many new people and developed new friendships
15. Joined a disaster relief group through my church
16. Hired a tutor in an attempt to learn Spanish
17. Taken up yoga
18. Written published articles for groups such as a nonprofit that is concerned with women's world issues and an organization that promotes lifestyles that support charities.
19. Participated in the planning of various fundraisers in Chicago, Los Angeles, and New York City

20. Had my story featured online: www.momversation.com/herstory/choosing-life-after-death

21. Continued to seek out God's will for my life by taking chances as I learn to experience greater peace in my life without Mark on this earth

22. Realized that there are many hurting people in this world and that we are called to use what we have and have experienced to help one another

Advice

People often ask for my advice when they encounter grief in their own life or in the life of someone they love. Perhaps my best advice for those wanting to support someone who is grieving is to humbly walk beside them. Reach out to them to let them know you are there in case they want to talk and then simply listen. Many are too quick to try to say something in an attempt to make it better, and their words can often be hurtful, even when the intentions are good. I remember finding the most comfort in the embrace of a friend who simply said, "There are no words," as she cried with me. I appreciated those who continually showed that they were there for me by calling and writing without expecting a response. They let me know that they were there in case I ever needed to talk. Although in the beginning I didn't return a number of calls or e-mails, I remember them. I remember my aunt who wrote postcards to me throughout the years following Mark's death. I remember my friends who left messages saying that they were praying for me and that I didn't need to call them back. I remember my family who came beside me in my grief and hardly said a word. I remember, and I am grateful—forever grateful.

Acknowledgements

Thank you—

To Jesus Christ, who has given all that is good. He gave me the strength and vision to publish this journal with the intent to help others who grieve. May they know that they are not alone.

To my parents, my sisters, and my brother-in-law Josh: You dropped everything to be with me in my darkest hours and to hold my hand as you helped lead me to lighter days. I love you more than words can express.

To John and Vicky: You have loved me like your own daughter and raised the wonderful man that I fell in love with. I love you.

To Mike: I had always wanted a brother, and I'm grateful for the time we spent together.

To Coffee: You faithfully supported the family as a friend and a pastor.

To Matt and Heather: We were blessed to have you as our MFC, and I will forever cherish the memories we had together. We have had the best of times and worst of times together. The bond I share with you is stronger than I could have ever imagined.

To Amy and Rick: Rick, thank you for sharing your wife with me. She has always been a light in my life, and our adventures together are treasures in my soul.

To Paige and Joe: I have so many amazing memories of our time together in Glen Ellyn. Mark and I felt so lucky to have you as neighbors and friends. Joe, thank you for mowing my lawn and taking care of my house during those years. Paige, your quiet wisdom has always impressed me and left me speechless in gratitude.

To Tony and Lek: Thank you for your friendship over the years. I have always known you were there to lend a hand when needed. Your servant hearts blow me away.

To Ben, Bill, Doug, Pete, Tony, and their wives: Thank you for remaining such great friends over the years.

To Nate: Thank you for listening, making me laugh, and calling me out for being a stoic Swede when needed.

To Kirsten: Thank you for living out the adventure of life with me in the years following Mark's death.

To Alana: Thank you for your friendship and free psychology sessions. Our discussions about what really matters in life coupled with laughter and dancing have always been just what the doctor ordered.

To Kelly and Erin: You are amazing women. I wish none of us knew the pain of being a widow, but I'm grateful that God gave us each other.

To Charity: My dear friend, you were there for me when I lost Mark, and now, unfortunately, I find that the favor needs to be returned. I love you.

To my business partner Tania: You've provided me with a new inspiration in life. This adventure that we are sharing together gives me such joy and purpose.

To Carole, Whitney, Justin, Paul, Erin, and the others from Park Church: You became such great friends in only a year's time.

To my coworkers at Corron Elementary: You showed such care and concern in my time of need and the years following. It was a blessing to have worked there.

To friends like Johnell, Dre, Amy, Alexis, Anna, Megan, Heidi, Ryan, and Jon: You showed up and supported me at unexpected times. Thank you.

To John: Thank you for being strong and confident enough to walk beside me and show me that there are possibilities for new beginnings. I respect and love the man you are.

To all my new friends who have supported me in this process and who have added joy to my life: Thank you.

Finally, to my late husband Mark: I will always be grateful for the time I had with you on this earth. I am a better person for having loved and been loved by you.

With a humble heart full of gratitude, I thank you all.

CPSIA information can be obtained at www.ICGtesting.com
Printed in the USA
LVOW071423010812

292534LV00015B/35/P